Agenda for Business and Higher Education

Business–Higher Education Forum

Edited by Thomas M. Stauffer

AMERICAN COUNCIL ON EDUCATION

© 1980 by American Council on Education
One Dupont Circle
Washington, D.C. 20036

Library of Congress Cataloging in Publication Data

American Council on Education. Business–Higher Education Forum.
  Agenda for Business and Higher Education.

  Proceedings of a meeting held Nov. 8–9, 1979, in
Washington.

  1. Industry and education—United States—
Congresses.   2. Industry and state—United States—
Congresses.   3. Education-Higher—economic aspects—
United States—Congresses.   4. Academic freedom—
Congresses.   I. Stauffer, Thomas M.   II. Title.
LC1085.A45   1980   378'.103   80-14352
ISBN 0-8268-1443-3

9 8 7 6 5 4 3 2 1

PRINTED IN THE UNITED STATES OF AMERICA

*The opinions and recommendations in this book are those of the authors
and are not intended to represent the official policy or endorsement of the
Business–Higher Education Forum or the American Council on Education.*

Contents

Foreword

ESTABLISHMENT OF THE BUSINESS–HIGHER EDUCATION FORUM IN 1978 represented a step toward closer cooperation and better understanding between two of the most important elements of American society: the corporation and the campus. The Forum is evidence that the academic community is increasingly concerned about many of the issues also on the agenda of corporate America: the health of our economy, the interrelations between research and development, the need to preserve appropriate autonomy for our businesses and institutions while insuring their responsiveness to social needs, and so forth. The Forum is based on the premise that by working together corporate and academic leaders can not only better educate themselves on how to deal with matters that come before them in the ordinary course of their duties, but also make contributions on issues before our nation.

Of course, contacts between business leaders and colleges and universities have long existed; business people have given generously of their time and money to our institutions. What distinguishes the Forum relationship from other points of contact—boards of trustees, advisory bodies, professional societies, recruiting efforts, and various more specific cooperative arrangements—is that it affords an opportunity at the highest corporate and institutional levels for exchange of views on matters that transcend single entities, no matter how far-flung their operations or size.

This volume represents an initial examination of some basic issues that received attention at recent Forum meetings.

J. W. PELTASON, *President*
American Council on Education

Agenda for Business and Higher Education

THOMAS M. STAUFFER

AMERICAN BUSINESS AND AMERICAN HIGHER EDUCATION, ESPECIALLY since World War II, have entered into a partnership. Business people are trustees of colleges and universities. They are alumni and parents of students. They serve on advisory bodies. There is the Conference Board, Joint Committee on Economic Education, Council for Financial Aid to Education, and other collaborative groups. Corporate and campus employees have contact through professional societies, business and technical training programs, job recruitment, summer visitations and exchanges, businessmen-in-residence programs and the contraposition. Then there are plant visits, scholarships, cooperative education, lifelong learning and career change, internships, colloquia and courses, curricular materials, contractual arrangements, and philanthropy, among other examples. There is joint activity in consultancies and speakers, in health and research programs, in education of corporate employees, and in management advice. Business has played a prominent role in the debate over the value of liberal arts and vocational/technical curricula. Higher education has been a source of fundamental research, expertise, and trained manpower, and business has provided the productive margin that has permitted colleges and universities to prosper.

Because the free-market economy and academic freedom have similar roots, there would seem to exist a reasonable basis for accommodation. Yet, clearly, each sector has a distinct point of view. Private enterprise fulfills its primary social function when it makes a profit; universities do so when they are sources of learning and criticism. Sometimes these two functions may conflict and misunderstanding or ill-will may well develop—the Vietnam War era is an obvious example. But, as Professor John Dunlop of Harvard, former Labor Secretary and advisor to presidents, has observed, differences between the

1

sectors need to be recognized and respected so that coalition building around a common agenda can take place.[1]

Since the early 1970s, relations between corporation and campus have been warming, in part from mutual enlightened self-interest. Students have demanded more relevance of the curriculum to their career intentions; college and university presidents have asked for more help, financial and in kind. Corporate executives, more and more frequently the product of graduate educations, have demonstrated appreciation for the powerful societal role universities play in teaching, research, and public service. Also, this coalition has been fostered by such influential phenomena as inflation, global interdependence, mass opinion, government regulation, and what has been called the postindustrial American economy. These are powerful forces upon which to unite. Furthermore, as Professor Dunlop has concluded, "America is a society of coalitions and both business and higher education need friends in society."[2]

BUSINESS–HIGHER EDUCATION FORUM

An important manifestation of this coalition is the Business–Higher Education Forum. Initiated by the American Council on Education— an independent, nonprofit higher education association and the nation's major coordinating body for colleges, universities, and related organizations—the Forum is part of higher education's effort to reach out to other segments of society: the media, government, labor, the military, women's and minority groups, and so on.

Inaugurated in 1978, the Forum by early 1980 included more than thirty chief executive officers of major corporations and a like number of college and university presidents and chancellors. The first meeting of the Forum convened in Williamsburg, Virginia, in late January 1979; the second in November 1979. Two meetings are to be scheduled each year. According to the founding document, the purposes of the Forum are

> (1) to be a contact point for the highest-ranking leaders of corporate America and American higher education for mutual material and in-

1. John Dunlop, remarks at meeting of the Business–Higher Education Forum, January 27, 1979, Williamsburg, Virginia.
2. Ibid.

Thomas M. Stauffer is director of the division of external relations, American Council on Education, and staff director of the Business–Higher Education Forum.

tellectual benefit; (2) to be a focal point . . . in which mutual appreciation of problems and needs will be advanced . . . ; (3) to advance mutual
understanding through an exchange of ideas and points-of-view at
periodic retreats and by other means; (4) to address problems shared
in common or held separately; and, when determined, to engage in
coordinated activity; and (5) to facilitate understanding of corporate
America on the campuses of the nation's colleges and universities.

In the future, Forum activity will probably center on policy issues
of national, even international, consequence and on business–higher
education interaction. This volume explores some of those issues.

THE WILLIAMSBURG MEETING

At the Forum's first meeting, in Williamsburg, "productivity, innovation, and research" was the principal agenda topic. The complexity
attending this topic was quickly revealed. Although time was inadequate, definitions imprecise, and trends difficult to measure, Forum
members reviewed the causes of the productivity lag. Participants
agreed that increased rates of innovation were a national priority.
Frank Press, White House science advisor, who also participated in
Williamsburg, noted President Carter's strong interest in the matter.

Although the Forum was not intended to address the productivity
question comprehensively, the link between university science and
industrial science was addressed. Members agreed that research was
only one factor, albeit influential, affecting the productivity rate. The
advantages of conducting scientific research in each sector thus far
have not been adequately understood or optimally related.

Misunderstandings existed in both sectors. Representatives from
universities and colleges seemed to lack sensitivity to the product and
manpower needs of industry and business, and their counterparts
from business and industry, in turn, did not seem to appreciate the
depth of such interest in the institutions, for example, the demands
by students for curricular relevance. Incentives for collaborative
projects, such as Route 128, "Silicon Valley," or Research Triangle
Park, needed to be made clear, and industry needed to help higher
education institutions understand industry's particular product needs,
especially its ability to innovate. Participants agreed that because
bureaucratic layers stifled innovation in both universities and industry, small-scale settings and climates for creative work must be found.
Providing incentives for resident scientists to pursue opportunities
should be encouraged.

3

Forum members agreed that our national economy was weakened and competitively threatened by the productivity lag and that our technological edge had diminished—even though there was a basis for genuine pride about much past and present accomplishment. Enlightened leadership is required to set things straight. Forum members also agreed that because they are uniquely situated to be advocates for solutions to problems, closer collaboration was essential on matters related to productivity, innovation, and research and to the impact of federal regulation on private-sector activity.

In addition to considering the building of a coalition around necessary leadership, the Forum also considered programming alternatives. Tax incentives to support research initiatives might be pursued, for example, although problems in obtaining Congressional support could not be discounted. With or without federal participation, however, the following possibilities remained: industrial commissioning of university research; jointly funded research; industry or industry-based centers for cooperative technology; demonstration of the effects of federal regulation and creative alternatives to regulation; a national advisory book on cooperative technology; a means for informing universities and industries of research manpower needs; targeting of money toward future industrial needs in research and innovation (a top priority is manufacturing technology); encouraging federal sources of seed money, matching grants, and low-interest loans; and finally, a mechanism for a two-way flow of personnel between the sectors for training and understanding. Forum members agreed that each of these possibilities merited serious attention.[3]

In preparation for its November 1979 meeting, in Scottsdale, Arizona, the Forum commissioned papers on eight topics: federal regulation, productivity, international business and international studies, energy research, engineering manpower, research and development, personnel exchanges, sharing expertise. These papers were the basis for the discussions. The first four papers are included in this volume to illustrate the business–higher education agenda.

Although there was unanimous agreement that the four papers should be published as a contribution to informed discussion and national debate, **members of the Forum made clear that publication did not imply their individual endorsement of every recommenda-**

3. Previously reported in Thomas M. Stauffer, "Expanding Business–Higher Education Cooperation on Research and Development," *Journal of the Society of Research Administrators*, Summer 1979, pp. 41–46.

tion made by the authors. The authors speak only for themselves. In fact, given the complexity of the issues, Forum members disagreed on many of the specific recommendations. Yet, the analyses were of a quality to merit wide distribution.

BUSINESS–HIGHER EDUCATION AGENDA

As already noted, business and higher education leaders have a mutual stake in issues of broad national consequence and in matters on the relationship between the sectors. A wide array of questions, not already noted, crowd the long-term agenda of the Forum and of business people and academicians generally. The agenda is impressive for its range and importance; opportunity is apparent. If leaders from both sectors approach the agenda in a spirit of constructive good will, their potential for influence over future directions of these issues is high. Such nongovernmental initiatives, especially at a time of criticism of governmental intervention in the private sector, should be encouraged.

Although the following list is not comprehensive, it does illustrate other issues of consequence, divided by general national interests and matters pertaining to the business–higher education relationship.

Mutual Policy Interests

- manpower planning
- the state of economic research and advice
- status of the professions
- academic freedom—economic freedom
- public policy involvement of executive officers
- national goals and response to social needs
- equality of opportunity
- public service options (taking over functions traditionally lodged in government agencies)
- youth policy
- structural change in American public systems
- national security imperatives
- research and development issues
- health education and policy
- limits or opportunities in growth
- ethics
- role of chief executive officers in their respective organizations

- community relations
- citizenship and responsibility
- economic policy
- private-public sector relations
- policy development and evaluation
- national leadership alliances
- aging of the population
- quality standards and recertification
- profit making and nonprofit differentiation
- legislative agenda

Specific Relationship Interests

- interdependence, dependence, and independence of American business and higher education
- corporate philanthropy
- quality of a college education
- business schools
- educational productivity and efficiency
- career versus general education
- adult and lifelong education
- business-academic colloquia
- education and training of leaders
- education for entrepreneurship
- economic literacy
- trusteeship/the board room
- business management techniques applied to academic administration
- cooperative research projects and technology transfer
- telecommunications use in higher education
- university education versus corporate-based education
- financial incentives in higher education
- managing college/university endowments
- education and training
- image of corporate America on campus
- inhibitors to college attendance
- business studies
- personnel exchanges
- international education
- employee motivation and personnel practices
- career education

- affirmative action
- athletics
- employee benefits

Federal regulation

The first four topics before the corporate and academic leaders in the Forum were federal regulation, productivity, energy research, and international relationships between business and higher education. Patrick M. Morgan, professor of political science, Washington State University, who previously worked on the problem for the Sloan Commission on Government and Higher Education through the University of California, Berkeley, was commissioned to write the paper on federal regulation.

The rapid expansion of federal regulation in recent years has had a well-publicized impact on both higher education and business. The problem has been debated almost endlessly in board rooms, on political platforms, and in the press. But the problems go far beyond determining the numbers that describe the costs or benefits.

Federal regulation poses many large problems and one especially large one. The "large" ones are familiar: reporting procedures, internal costs, frustrations and delay, inflation, and second-order and unintended consequences of individual regulations. All are difficult and irritating but surmountable in degree. The even larger problem, though, is federal intrusion, both into state and local governments and into nongovernmental areas and institutions, on such a scale as to threaten the autonomy of private functions in the United States.

In some ways, regulation is a peculiarly American problem because, to an unusual extent, American society was constructed on the premise that major activities need to be operated apart from government. Because government does not operate industries, business, or other institutions, it has to regulate—the very idea of regulation implies continued separate existence of broad segments of society beyond the government. However, this proposition is being nibbled away as more and more nongovernmental institutions are becoming dependent on government. The worry is that no one has a broad administrative grasp on the entire situation.

To date, the political and philosophical roots of the administrative problem have been overlooked in addressing this issue. The overriding question is, To what extent and for what purposes do we want the

7

government to compromise the autonomy of economic, educational, and other institutions, and how can we arrange to have regulations carry intrusion no further than those overriding purposes require? The Congress and the White House need a standard against which to evaluate demands for further regulation and to assess specific types of existing regulation. Almost certainly the answer will have to be developed by those who are regulated and then advocated in convincing fashion through the political process. Otherwise, the "answer" will emerge by default and will reflect the administrative and political convenience of those doing the regulating. Morgan reviews proposals for reform and then recommends standards against which federal regulation should be measured.

At the Scottsdale meeting, consensus was substantial that federal regulation in many areas had become excessive and stifling of the private sector. Regulation has become an adversarial process because regulators, perhaps going beyond Congressional intent, have stressed what may be technically feasible rather than what is always sensible. Moreover, regulators promote single-interest structures that do not consider competing values and trade-offs. Excessive regulation, for example, is a major factor in the declining national productivity rate.

Several "fixes" for this dilemma were recommended and discussed. Requiring Congress to approve all regulations is one possibility. An annual "regulatory budget" prepared to indicate costs and benefits is another, as is a high-level, quasi-independent review of regulations and recommended changes. Any one of these possibilities, perhaps in combination with others, would dramatize the costs and the benefits of regulation to society, hopefully striking a safe balance.

Self-regulation was discussed as a long-term alternative. Although great hope was expressed for this possibility, the Forum noted that examples of self-regulatory failure abound, too. Bar associations, medical societies, and college faculties, for example, have not demonstrated eagerness to discipline the professionally weak among them.

That there is a role for regulation in American society, as underscored in the Morgan paper, was acknowledged. In an era of accountability and consumerism, regulation is the inevitable outcome. The degree of regulation was the only question. Regulatory standards are often far more negative, contradictory, and punitive than they need to be; self-regulation deserves more attention, as does setting of positive performance standards.

Productivity

Professor John W. Kendrick of George Washington University and the University of Hawaii-Manoa, a national authority on productivity, was commissioned to consider the range of options available to improve the productive capacity of the American economy, including those in which business and higher education might have mutual interest. His survey resulted in the presentation of ninety-nine options, or recommendations.

The dominant role of total capital formation in productivity growth stands out in the discussion. It accounted for three-fourths of the growth of output per unit of labor input in 1948–66, and, because the net effect of the other factors was negative, *more than* all of it after 1966. "Total" capital formation includes not only the conventional tangible investments in structures, equipment, inventories and natural resources development, but also the "intangible" (non-material) investments in R&D, education and training, health and safety, and mobility. The complementarity of the various types of investment is high. R&D raises rates of return on and demand for tangible capital goods in which it is embodied, and the tangibles help diffuse new technology. Education prepares the scientists, engineers, and managers who invent and innovate, while technological progress creates demand for more highly educated and trained persons. Better health increases the return on education, while the educational sector plays an important role in medical research and in diffusing health information. Mobility is essential for the economy to adapt to and maximize the return on new technology. When one form of investment lags, as has R&D in the past decade, the effectiveness of other types is reduced.

Kendrick suggests a two-pronged approach to reaccelerating the growth of the real capital stocks per unit of labor by raising investment rates: first, he calls for reasonably steady, predictable, and significant rates of increase in public investments; and second, he proposes various tax and other incentives to spur private business and personal investments in these areas. He notes that, at relatively high employment, measures to increase saving would be needed to permit noninflationary further expansion of investments and to help hold down interest rates. And, with respect to tangible investment, he points out that measures to accelerate productivity and reduce relative prices of capital goods stimulate investment. The same holds

9

true of capital services. Another theme that informed much of the discussion was reliance on the market-pricing system.

Readers should note that the proposed tax measures are designed primarily to offset the anti-saving/investment bias of the present tax system. That is, people would save and invest more if government did not reduce rates of return to savers and investors through income and related taxes.

The various policy directions followed in Kendrick's paper may suggest some ambivalence toward the role of government. But Kendrick does not believe this to be the case—he recognizes the legitimate functions of government and advocates only that they be performed more effectively and efficiently, which means accentuating the positive and minimizing the negative. In addition to proposals for mitigating negative impacts of taxes, he makes a host of specific recommendations for reform of both economic and social regulations to reduce their unfavorable impact on productivity while still seeking to effectuate their socially mandated objectives. Although some trade-off may be necessary, he believes it can be tilted more in favor of the productivity goal.

Most individuals and groups will probably agree on the general nature and thrust of most of the policy initiatives Kendrick proposes. Some will undoubtedly disagree with some of the specific tax reform and expenditure proposals, especially the idea of using a value-added tax as a means of recouping revenue losses from reduction of income taxes. But it can be surmised that the increases in aggregate supply and demand that would result from a program of the sort proposed would increase tax revenues from existing sources sufficiently to make up much of the initial reduction in revenue from the recommended tax cuts. It is also clear that a productivity-enhancing program of legislation would have to be phased in gradually as economic, budgetary, and political conditions permit.

Kendrick presents a broad "menu" of policy options, rather than suggesting specific policy measures on which the business and higher education sections could agree and on which joint action might be taken. In any case, such measures would have to emerge from joint discussions, for which this paper and others will serve as background. Addendum A of Kendrick's paper discusses areas of special concern. Addendum B examines recent proposals of the Carter Administration on productivity.

The discussion at Scottsdale concerned ways the United States could reverse the decline in its productivity rate. Forum members agreed that the Kendrick paper on productivity was a reasoned, encyclopedic review of measures that could be taken in the United States to stem the slide in the productivity rate. The question at this session was not one of lack of options but one of national will to enact necessary measures. Caveats were expressed, however, as follows: because the paper is so encyclopedic, those parts that constitute acceptable and politically viable packages of reforms must be highlighted, and priorities must be set among the recommendations; what the private sector needs to do requires emphasis, thus relegating the federal government to a court of second resort; tough trade-offs, it must be understood, would have to be made among the ninety-nine recommendations.

Forum members agreed on broad, basic principles for cooperative activity between the sectors. They agreed that business and higher education leaders must avoid expressing the conventional wisdom of despair about American productivity—otherwise there is a danger of being caught in a self-fulfilling prophecy about America's future. They agreed that national income growth and productivity increase can be sustained at reasonable and responsible levels if correct policies are adopted—such growth is a viable *policy option* on resource use, federal government role, and national mood. Both higher education and business members agreed that high growth rates in productivity will come primarily through increased rates of savings and capital formation, sensible limits to federal regulation and spending, and increased attention to research and development. Further, they agreed that federal policies *can* be adjusted to improve capital formation; that cost-benefit criteria need to be established for justifying the level of federal regulation; that a sense of national urgency or crisis exists for improving the productivity rate; that such improvement is an imperative for business, higher education, and the nation; and that the times are right to press actions to improve the rate.

Energy research

On August 15, 1979, President David S. Saxon of the University of California commissioned a paper "on the role of research in energy policy, the roles of universities and other performers in achieving research objectives, and on mechanisms that the United States should

11

employ to implement new university energy research programs."[4] Saxon did so as chairman of the Committee on Science and Research of the Association of American Universities (AAU), the organizational affiliation of the major research institutions in the United States and Canada. Professor Jack M. Hollander of Lawrence Berkeley Laboratory was invited to head an AAU Energy Advisory Committee to make recommendations. Members of the advisory committee are listed in Hollander's paper.

President Saxon's initiative came at the request of White House domestic policy and science advisors, respectively, Stuart Eizenstat and Frank Press. They asked the AAU "to propose to them how universities might organize and develop their programs of research to best contribute to solving the nation's energy needs." Eizenstat and Press specifically asked that universities not propose "more of the same," but instead asked for "new ideas, for new approaches, and for new mechanisms."[5]

The report recommends a long-range strategy for energy research emphasizing "goal-oriented basic research," education of scientists to meet future needs, and mechanisms for universities, industry, and government. Under the plan, university energy research centers would be established with support of the federal government, each having a goal and multidisciplinary orientation. These centers would be the university base for cooperative programs with federal laboratories and industry. As the report states, "Each member of this unique American 'research triangle' has important contributions to make to the work of the others, and an enhanced symbiotic relationship among [industry, universities, and federal laboratories] will substantially increase the effectiveness of the entire national energy program."

University energy research centers, selected on the basis of a national competition following reviews by government, academic, and industrial leaders, are advocated. Start-up costs would include equipment and instrumentation. Each center would have an advisory council, composed of representatives of universities, industry, national laboratories, and state and local governments, to make recommendations to the research center and the U.S. Department of Energy. These centers (ideally ten to fifteen) would also benefit from a national

4. Letter from Jack M. Hollander, Chairman, AAU Energy Advisory Committee, to President David S. Saxon, University of California, September 21, 1979.
5. Letter from President David S. Saxon, University of California, to members of the Business–Higher Education Forum, October 24, 1979.

energy support program. Included would be project research support (funded on a peer-review competitive basis), traineeships and fellowships, challenge grants, and a national advisory commission.

At the Scottsdale meeting, the Forum agreed that the energy crisis is the greatest threat to the nation since World War II. But unlike wars, which are usually crises of limited duration, the energy crisis must be thought of in terms of decades, a long-term struggle. American leaders and experts are stymied and frustrated in approaching the energy dilemma; this will continue until there is grass-roots acceptance that a crisis really exists. Besides the political problems, the priorities for dealing with the energy crisis also include improvement of efficiency, movement on planned or stalled projects, adoption of new technologies, and expansion of long-term research and development.

Early involvement of industry is crucial. Some models of university-industry collaboration were mentioned, including Cornell University's microprocessing technology transfer facility and the old National Advisory Committee for Aeronautics. The multidisciplinary emphasis in the proposal needs to be emphasized.

The AAU proposal, the Forum concluded, is clearly a good start in getting universities more involved in solving the nation's energy problem. The proposal will signal the importance of closer university-industry cooperation on research and of more goal-oriented, interdisciplinary basic research.

International business and international studies

Drs. Samuel L. Hayden of the Council of the Americas and Leslie W. Koepplin of Rutgers—The State University of New Jersey were commissioned to consider linkages between foreign market interests of major corporations and international studies programs on American campuses. Previously in 1979, they were requested to make recommendations on this subject to the President's Commission on Foreign Language and International Studies.

They concluded that, except for a few noteworthy examples, communications on the international interests of universities and corporations have been lacking. Effective and pervasive working relationships have been precluded largely because of a lack of knowledge of the role and motivating factors of each set of principals. But improvements are likely if the mutual international interests of corporation and campus are better understood.

13

Some 250 firms account for roughly 80 percent of U.S. exports. Their size is such that the majority belongs to the "Fortune 500" list with annual sales in the hundreds of millions of dollars. For many, international markets are the future growth areas. However, these multinational firms, although having several features in common, are not monolithic or uniform in behavior. For example, some relatively new-to-international-market financial institutions are forecasting tremendous growth overseas, while more experienced banks are seeing a leveling off of growth; some firms are seeking efficiency through integrated operations worldwide, while others are seeking resources; some are predominantly exporters from the United States, while others manufacture in host country markets to service local consumption or for export to Third-World countries; some are mainly exporters, while others are direct investors. Often, large individual firms incorporate many of these characteristics of behavior simultaneously. In addition, sectoral differences occur whereby engineering and construction firms have different concerns and behavior than do service, agribusiness, or manufacturing firms. These differences extend to geographical regions. Some 80 percent of the total U.S. direct investment abroad of $165 billion is in OECD countries. There is comparatively little activity in Africa, and business in the U.S.S.R. has not reached the predicted potential. These differences are seemingly rarely appreciated by groups outside the corporate community.

In personnel terms, the route to overseas work is often through the domestic corporate structure. It is rare indeed for recent university graduates to enter an international position. There is, therefore, little demand for international studies or foreign language skills that are unrelated to business education. And, because U.S. multinationals have a good record of promoting host-country nationals to responsible managerial positions, the demand for U.S. trained international experts is somewhat further dampened. This is certainly why many U.S. firms look to—and often track—foreign students on U.S. campuses. For corporate employees assigned abroad, cultural and linguistic skills, although recognized as important, usually are secondary to product and organizational knowledge. The development of cross-cultural skills is a function of time and is often left to on-the-job efforts.

Despite what some would term a rather dismal picture of U.S. myopia, U.S. multinationals have fared well against increased competition abroad. Several questions need to be raised, however. For example, how much more effective would U.S. international firms be if their employees had cross-cultural training that matched their managerial training? How much more important will the cultural aspects be as business diplomacy becomes more a fact of life? With the reduction of U.S. bilateral assistance abroad and with multilateralization on the rise, to what extent will U.S. business interests become a surrogate for nonexistent government programs? How will U.S. firms cope effectively with the rise of foreign state enterprises, and who will service the U.S. managerial need for more constructive business-government relations at home and abroad? And finally, as U.S. business interests continue to grow overseas, to what extent should U.S. firms assume some major responsibility for international education at home?

Five characteristics of international studies on campuses must be understood before examining proposals on how to improve corporate-campus linkage: (1) America's international studies capacities are relatively new—most date from only the early 1960s; (2) there has been a lack of funds for curriculum innovation involving these new resources; (3) most of these international studies resources are concentrated in humanities and social sciences, with notable weaknesses in economics and certain of the professional schools, including business and management; (4) the internal campus reward system does not encourage communication among the humanities and social sciences, schools of business and international business; and (5) there are some problems within the schools of business regarding international business education.

Specific proposals are made in the paper: the first includes ways to increase the level of resources available for international education; and the second recommends three project proposals as part of an action agenda in the international area. The underlying assumption of the proposals is that closer collaboration between higher education and private enterprise will be to the advantage of each and will be in the national interest.[6]

At Scottsdale, discussion demonstrated relatively weak appreciation by Forum-member educators for the international business needs of American corporations and by business leaders for the international

---

6. Portions of some summary statements on the papers were extracted from executive summaries prepared by the authors of the papers.

studies programs of universities. Hope was expressed that publication of the recent report of the President's Commission on Foreign Languages and International Studies and directions set by the Business–Higher Education Forum would strengthen mutual understanding and spur cooperation.

Educators noted their interest in the language and cross-cultural training needs of American corporations. Also noted were business–higher education collaboration for creation of business schools abroad; recruitment of the highest quality foreign students, perhaps through better availability of fellowships; training of the ablest transnational talent and concentrating on leadership and managerial training; adequacy of education in the role of American multinational corporations, whose activities in dollar terms outweigh U.S. government activity abroad roughly by twenty-five times; and the need for business to help higher education understand its requirements in international studies.

Forum-member business leaders highlighted their practical needs in operating internationally. Business use of crash courses for foreign language training, rather than the universities; business needs for training indigenous managers, not Americans; and the interest of business in operating stable, prosperous foreign markets were highlighted. All in all, business leaders voiced their sense that American universities were generally not well attuned to their special requirements, although interest in exploring possibilities for practical exchanges remained.

FORUM PAPERS

The four papers that follow not only illustrate the business–higher education agenda, but also stand on their merits as useful discussions of diverse issues. Thus, the papers are addressed to diverse communities involved in national policy making and opinion shaping. The paper on federal regulation has applicability to debates in the Congress and the White House, and in the platform committees of the major political parties. The productivity paper will be of interest to economists and policy makers alike, while the paper on energy research will draw the attention of the scientific community and agencies of the federal government. The final paper addresses problems limited more to interests of internationalists in corporations and on campuses.

The Business–Higher Education Forum members asked that these papers be circulated to policy makers and relevant communities. To reiterate a previous caveat, though, the thoughts and recommendations expressed by the authors do not necessarily represent the opinions of individual Forum members. The issues are complex and opinions vary. Comments to the Business–Higher Education Forum of the American Council on Education are invited.

Federal Regulation:
Problems and Solutions

PATRICK M. MORGAN

THIS PAPER DESCRIBES THE PROBLEM OF FEDERAL REGULATION OF BUSI-
ness and higher education, reviews efforts to deal with the problem,
examines suggestions for reform, and evaluates where to go from
here. The term "regulation" is used loosely, in many places, to refer
to any and all of the following: laws passed to control the operation
of various sectors of society; regulations promulgated by executive
agencies to implement such laws, forms, and reports those agencies
require from the citizenry; enforcement procedures used by those
agencies; and the paperwork, complications, and delays that naturally
accompany all these things.

Not the least of the burdens of federal regulations is the proliferation of discussion about it. New books on regulation appear every
month; the journals are full of papers on it; the newspapers and
magazines run articles on the revolt against regulation; Congress is
spewing out reports and hearings; the executive branch is studying
and restudying the problem; even Common Cause has taken it up.
Some battles are being won, but the war is being lost. In fact, it appears that the war cannot be won, for good reasons—"good" in the
sense that they are understandable and there is need to come to
terms with them. All that follows is infused by this view and is an
explication of it.

THE PROBLEM

There has been an explosive growth in federal regulation in recent
decades, regulation that intrudes deeply into the operation of business and higher education organizations, among others, and that
imposes strains, costs, and other burdens of varying severity. The
Federal Register had 16,000 pages in 1966; it is expected to hit

18

100,000 in the next year or two. To take just one period, 1970–75, the number of pages in the *Code of Federal Regulations* grew by more than 30 percent. During those years seven major new regulatory agencies were created, and some thirty major new laws with regulatory impact were passed.[1] As of 1976, more than eighty federal agencies were engaged in regulation of some sort.[2] Regulation of business is an old story, although it has greatly expanded in recent years, but regulation of higher education has only a brief history and yet it too has mushroomed. Today there are more than 400 laws affecting postsecondary education, overseen by some thirty-four committees and seventy or more subcommittees of Congress and administered by a multitude of agencies. In 1964 such laws ran to ninety pages; now they exceed 360 pages. Laws mean regulations—ninety-two pages worth in the 1965 *Federal Register* and nearly 1,000 pages in 1977.[3] Two hundred thousand people in the executive branch are needed to manage the entire regulatory complex and the more than five thousand different government forms people fill out each year. And regulatory agencies themselves cost money—more than $4 billion a year and rising.[4]

There are also thousands of regulations pertaining to each major industry, such as steel or drugs, and these regulations call for prodigious amounts of paperwork to be filled out and returned before a TV license can be renewed, a new drug approved for public consumption, or a new refinery built.

1. William Lilley III and James Miller III, "The New 'Social Regulation,'" *The Public Interest*, No. 47 (Spring 1977), pp. 49–52.

2. Charles Schultze, *The Public Use of Private Interest* (Washington: The Brookings Institution, 1977), p. 7.

3. *The Entangling Web: Federal Regulation of Colleges and Universities*, Editorial Projects for Education Special Report to Alumni/ae 1979 (Providence, Rhode Island: Editorial Projects for Education, 1979).

4. *The Regulatory Reform Act of 1977, Hearings Before the Subcommittee on Intergovernmental Relations of the Committee on Governmental Affairs, United States Senate* (Washington: Government Printing Office, 1977), pp. 4, 8. Also "New Federal Budget Calls For More Regulators," *Regulation*, March/April 1978, pp. 6–7; and Murray Weidenbaum, *The Future of Business Regulation* (New York: Amacom, 1979), p. 15.

Patrick M. Morgan is professor of political science at Washington State University.

The opinions and recommendations in this paper are those of the author and are not intended to represent the official policy or endorsement of the Business–Higher Education Forum or the American Council on Education.

Government regulation is as old as the government, and attempts to deal with it are not new.[5] It is the recent dimensions regulation has assumed—in density and in scope—that now provoke cries of alarm. The initial wave of regulations was a response to populist pressures and corruptions of the robber baron era before the turn of the century —the best example being regulation of the railroads. A second was a response to the Depression, and once again its focus was mainly on economic activities. The third wave began in the 1960s, swelled in the 1970s, and may not have crested yet. Some of this third-wave regulation is also economic in the sense that it tries to hold down health-care costs, inhibit mergers, or contain unscrupulous firms and fly-by-night colleges. But most of it is "social regulation" that seeks to end discrimination, clean up the environment, eliminate unsafe products and working conditions, and curb dangerous products. It is very consumer-oriented in many cases and is often designed to protect people from themselves. It is pervasive, injecting government into the detailed operations of state and local governments, firms, universities, and other organizations to a degree never before attempted in our history. Some regulation accompanies federal subsidies, favors, and benefits, while some stands alone. Hardly any of it seems to be simple.

In a democratic system, the government is entitled to some control over how tax money is to be spent. Expenditures and regulations frequently have laudable aims. In the higher education community the benefits from federal money are substantial, and support for the broad liberal economic and social goals of regulation is pervasive. Yet the criticisms of how the government operates have been steadily mounting in education and nearly everywhere else. Critics focus on the costs and burdens, not just the benefits, and the complaints have become so widespread and intense in the past four or five years that Washington officials have been forced to give serious consideration to reform.

Regulation poses many large problems, with one of particular significance. Among the former is the cost: regulation costs money. The direct administrative costs for federal agencies of more than $4 billion a year is just the start. The agencies make costly work for

5. For instance, the Federal Reports Act of 1942. See *History of Paperwork Reform Efforts, A Report of the Commission on Federal Paperwork* (Washington: Commission on Federal Paperwork, 1977).

those they regulate—filling out forms, submitting reports, doing repairs, installing new hiring procedures and grievance mechanisms, paying higher wages and legal costs, hiring more people, using more expensive production processes, even making trips to meetings to talk about regulation. Often regulation of firms curbs market forces that would otherwise drive prices of goods and services down. How much does all this regulation cost? Some estimates are $50–60 billion a year. The Federal Paperwork Commission and others put the bill at more than $100 billion.[6] Nobody knows for sure.

Another large problem is frustration, delays, and insecurity about whether or not one is in compliance. Sometimes the government seems to go out of its way to muddy instructions, complicate forms, duplicate requests and requirements, and demand mountains of unnecessary data. Confusions abound from incredibly detailed and obtuse regulations, shifting interpretations and rulings, and frequent changes in direction. The Occupational Safety and Health Administration (OSHA) and the Environmental Protection Agency (EPA) are favorite targets.

Another problem is the slow pace at which the government works. Delays in getting approval of projects in the field of energy are now getting special attention, but numerous instances exist elsewhere. Two years or more is not uncommon as the time it takes to get decisions out of regulatory agencies. Universities often get contract and grant awards or renewals well after the projected date or the onset of their academic or fiscal years. Of course, many of these delays are produced by the impact of the bureaucracy, and many officials themselves are frustrated by the delays. At one point the Office of Civil Rights had a backlog of 130,000 complaints to investigate, which that agency and others had done much to incite.

Finally, laws and regulations frequently have harmful unintended consequences or imposed burdens that do little to solve the problems that evoked them. Workplace accidents seldom result from the deficiencies OSHA insists on correcting at everyone's expense. New hiring practices mandated under affirmative action do not enlarge the pool of qualified applicants. Many of the regulations appear to excessively

---

6. *Final Summary Report, A Report of the Commission on Federal Paperwork* (Washington: Commission on Federal Paperwork, 1977), p. 5; Murray Weidenbaum, "On Estimating Regulatory Costs," *Regulation,* May/June 1978, pp. 14–17. Also Weidenbaum, op. cit. pp. 11–32.

restrict competition and thereby subsidize inefficiency; regulation often slows the pace of innovation and new investment, hampering economic growth and promoting inflation.

On balance these problems do not seem to be overwhelming, which is one reason for the difficulty in getting Washington's attention when objecting to them. Many of the estimated man-hours spent in filling out forms are for relatively simple or repetitive forms needed to obtain a particular subsidy or benefit, like a pension. Firms can pass many of the costs along to consumers, and some of the others can be absorbed. In a few cases the government underwrites some of the costs. In many cases, the costs come to far less than the benefits flowing to the institution from federal subsidies, contracts, and grants. Many regulated firms have in fact grown comfortable with regulation, whatever its costs, and now resist attempts to eliminate it. Few firms and educational institutions would readily exchange the benefits for an end to regulation.

Certain costs and problems are unavoidable. If corporation and university presidents are to be believed, they are not against safety or equal opportunity or cleaning up the environment. That being the case, they would have had to invest some resources on these matters anyway. Some of the problems of government are simply the problems of modern life; firms and educational institutions are slow at times, and so is the whole society. Complexity pervades daily activities in almost every way. Undoubtedly regulation contributes to inflation, but plenty of other things do as well. Thus we live every day with complexity and its frustrations, inflation and its effects, bureaucracy and its annoyances—regulation is more of the same and manageable as such.

The one regulation problem of particular significance is federal intrusion into local life. One element is the increasing penetration of state and local governments by Washington, undermining the federalism that is a cornerstone of our political system.[7] Another is government intrusion into nongovernmental areas and institutions on such a scale as to severely compromise the autonomy of major seg-

7. See Paul Posner and Stephen Sorett, "A Crisis in The Fiscal Commons: The Impact of Federal Expenditures on State and Local Governments," *Public Contract Law Journal*, Vol. 10, No. 2 (Winter 1978), pp. 341–377; and *Impact of Federal Paperwork on State and Local Governments: An Assessment by the Academy for Contemporary Problems, A Report to the Commission on Federal Paperwork* (Washington: Commission on Federal Paperwork, 1977).

ments of society. In some ways regulation is a peculiarly American problem because, to an unusual extent, this society is constructed on the premise that major activities need to be operated apart from the government. The state does not manage communications or run higher education. There is no state church. Most industrial, financial, and other businesses are privately owned and operated. The government has to *regulate* precisely because it does not *operate*. The very idea of regulation implies the continued separate existence of broad segments of society beyond the government. Regulation is used to enhance the general welfare, but self-regulation and self-operation of many aspects of our society are assumed to do the same.

We have been nibbling away at this proposition, and we are in danger of nibbling it to death. More and more nongovernmental institutions are financially dependent on the government or precariously close to being so. We are busily constructing a network of regulations that constrain their autonomy still more. Usually the regulations not only define expected results, but also means and procedures to be used to obtain those results. In their insistence on having things done their way, and by manipulating the financial dependence just referred to, government agencies are forcing many subtle, and often not so subtle, shifts in the priorities, operations, and procedures of those they regulate.

The problem has come upon us piecemeal, for there has been no underlying philosophy or general policy on governmental regulation. Individual statutes have created myriads of agencies, each doing its own thing, without any central guidance and direction. No one in the government has a broad administrative grasp of the entire situation. In regulation, there is not one government in Washington but innumerable little governments that rarely talk to each other.

This milieu helps to explain why there is little or no meaningful and lasting reform. The Carter Administration, like its predecessor, has resolutely attempted to do something, mainly working through the Office of Management and Budget. The difficulty is that the problem is always cast in *administrative* terms—get fewer forms, eliminate burdensome requirements, cut out duplication—when the essence of the problem is *political* and *philosophical*. The really significant question is: to what extent and for what purposes do we want the government to compromise the autonomy of economic, educational, and other institutions, and how can we arrange to have regulation

23

that carries intrusion no further than those overriding purposes require? A clear answer from the Administration and the Congress would provide a standard against which to evaluate demands for further regulation—which will assuredly arise—and to assess the utility of specific types of regulation. Almost certainly, the answer is going to have to be developed primarily by those who are the subject of regulation, then sold in convincing fashion through the political process, and finally supported by the voting public. Otherwise, the "answer" will emerge by default and will reflect what is administratively and politically expedient for the government and politically responsive to the pressures of those seeking the regulations in the first place.

THE POLITICAL–BUREAUCRATIC ROOTS
OF REGULATION

If there is a single underlying theme in complaints about regulation, it is bewilderment—the how-can-the-government-do-such-things attitude. This bewilderment is understandable if how the government works is considered. Knowing how the system functions can provide a guide both to the origins of regulation and to the solutions to the problems encountered.

There have been some basic shifts in our political system. One is the emergence of clusters of relatively intense single-interest groups dedicated to the pursuit of particular goals. These groups are extremely active in pressuring officials, generating media attention, and using the courts to enforce their preferences. Such groups do not tackle the political process in a spirit of compromise and coalition, for they think more in terms of adversarial relationships. They have helped make increasingly difficult the building of broad coalitions by politicians for electoral or legislative purposes, which has contributed to the continuing decline of American political parties and has made it just that much more difficult for Congress to conduct its business in the public interest. American politics has become severely fragmented as particular groups demand specific solutions to their problems. The volume of legislation has grown and with it the proliferation of individual agencies whose mission is to focus on one specific problem. The statutes, the new agencies, and the regulations reflect the adversarial spirit in which they were conceived. Behind each lies the presumption that the targets of regulation will not be amenable to doing the "right" thing, but must be forced into it.

Another major change in the political system is a declining inclination to be "practical" in the classic sense of counting the costs. The people pushing regulation do not see it as unduly costly or burdensome in comparison with the problems to be solved. Where safety or health or discrimination is involved, the economic costs are found to be irrelevant. Other values are more important than money or administrative convenience or autonomy. In 1976 the Council on Wage and Price Stability recommended abandoning proposed Labor Department regulations to eliminate cancer-causing emissions from coke ovens in the steel industry. The costs would have been $240 million a year to save an estimated 27 cancer deaths a year, some $9 million a life, and the Council suggested that more lives could be saved by spending that money somewhere else. The United Steel Workers Union described the recommendation as a "despicable" effort at "putting dollars ahead of human values."[8] Such views lend a strongly moral and adversarial tone to public debate; their advocates find opponents morally unworthy, in a sense, for adhering to values that are improper because they neglect paramount human concerns. Complaints about the costs and other difficulties involved tend to confirm their suspicions that the important human values will be ignored in the absence of detailed supervision.

This kind of debate is a natural development in an affluent society. The whole point to becoming affluent is to be able to ignore purely instrumental considerations, to be able to buy things we want irrespective of what we really "need" in the strict sense. Until recently the primary effect of this sort emerging from our affluence was conspicuous consumption of consumer luxuries. Putting our riches to more noble purposes was bound to become an issue.

To social reformers, the proper solution is usually law: make certain things illegal and coerce the violators. Such groups have little inclination to support subsidies to meet the costs of compliance, for that is simply rewarding the violators for behaving correctly now and for having misbehaved in the past. That is why law and regulation are advocated over using politics to create positive incentives to alter behavior.

8. Robert Kagan, *Regulatory Justice* (New York: Russell Sage Foundation, 1978), p. 10.

A third major change is an altered conception of the relationship between personal rights and the government. Our tradition has been to conceive of rights as something enjoyed against the government; to preserve and expand individual rights has usually meant putting restrictions on public authorities. Action by government to solve problems, in many cases, was a last resort, not an obvious first step. Our contemporary concerns are with rights of a sort that are threatened by someone other than the government—racists, polluters, producers of unsafe products. The government is not seen as the major threat but rather as an ally; what is sought is not further restriction of the government but the expansion of its power and activities. Elements of this change first appeared many years ago on economic matters and contributed to the emergence of the modern welfare state, and the change has accelerated in the past two decades.[9] Our traditional *fear* of government has become something approximating an *annoyance*.

That traditional view of rights is not easily reconciled with current concerns. Today's agenda for government action is awkwardly grafted onto a political system that grew out of a preoccupation with containing the government, producing a necessarily clumsy and unwieldly arrangement. Government is expanded but hedged all around by specifying its allowable actions in great detail in legislation or by requiring elaborate procedural mechanisms to keep the government from trampling on the citizenry.[10] By such means the trampling is not fully prevented, just drawn out—the trampling comes in slow motion.

To this is added the fact that in a fragmented system the welfare functions of the government are similarly fragmented as elected officials see to it that their constituents get a piece of the action. Compassion for the disadvantaged gets diluted by interest group pressures and Congressional politics, producing a tax system with staggering complexity and subtle inequities, and welfare programs that distribute rather broadly the benefits originally meant to assist those truly in need—the Law Enforcement Assistance Administration is a good case in point. It is no wonder that federal programs never die or even fade away.

9. Many elements of this description of American politics are detailed in Theodore Lowi, *The End of Liberalism*, 2nd Edition (New York: W. W. Norton, 1979).

10. A good discussion of this is Richard Stewart, "The Reformation of American Administrative Law," *Harvard Law Review*, Vol. 88, No. 8 (June 1975).

The pressure from special interests on the elected representative is relentless, bringing the constant danger of alienating too many and thereby damaging his reelection chances. The most obvious recourse is to legislate, which allows officials to demonstrate they are doing something. When support for a particular action appears strong or where the opportunities appear good to exploit public concern and media attention, legislators will spin out detailed statutes describing exactly what should be done, and how, and by when. In this way Congress is often the ultimate source of federal paperwork and red tape when it pushes through exceedingly fine-grained statutes specifying stringent reporting and record-keeping requirements, setting unreasonable deadlines, and requesting elaborate new studies. The then Secretary of HEW Joseph Califano once pointed to an education program passed by Congress "which requires us to write 90 regulations in 240 days and sets the exact date on which each regulation has to be issued."[11] Energy legislation passed in 1978 covers some 300 pages. And Congress, it appears, was the culprit behind the many burdens associated with Employee Retirement Income Security Act.

Even more common is the statute that goes in the opposite direction, ceding enormous responsibility to the bureaucracy by setting goals and defining what is to be done only in the vaguest of terms. When the statutes are vague, regulations may depart from Congressional intent, go far beyond it, or even contravene it (as in the use of quotas in managing armative action). More importantly, a statute is often responsive to the unwritten rule of American politics, in Charles Schultze's words, to "do no direct harm" to any significant group.[12] Political heat from any harm done is at least partly deflected onto the bureaucrats, who do not have to run for office after all. Congress can assert that something must be done, such as cutting automobile pollution, and then the manufacturers can wrestle with the bureaucrats to get regulations they feel they can live with.[13] When complaints necessarily arise, Congressmen have endless opportunities to intervene on behalf of constituents, to investigate abuses, to seek reforms, and to pose as opponents of bureaucracy. All this can

11. *The Role of Congress, A Report of the Commission on Federal Paperwork* (Washington: Commission on Federal Paperwork, 1977), p. 12.
12. Schultze, op. cit. pp. 23–25, 70–72.
13. See the discussion in Howard Margolis, "The Politics of Auto Emissions," *The Public Interest,* No. 49 (Fall 1977), pp. 3–21.

be parlayed into the votes necessary to be able to go on legislating indefinitely.

Congress is also directly responsible for much of the overlapping and duplication in federal programs. Power in Congress rests in the committees and subcommittees, which in turn derive power from their control over pieces of the government. To consolidate agencies and programs is to take away some Congressional turf, which is always vigorously resisted.

In the executive branch, regulation is also shaped by and responsive to the needs of bureaucrats irrespective of its impact on the general public. An initial point of departure is the fact that most regulation-minded agencies are relatively single-purpose in nature. Their employees are usually professionals who like their work and believe in what they are doing. They are not paid or otherwise motivated to do complex analyses of the impact of their regulations nor to subtly weigh the costs and goals involved against society's other values and concerns.

Regulation is also an exercise in bureaucratic self-protection. The strong disinclination in our political system to grant officials great autonomy and discretion, for fear that this would allow public power to be used for private benefit, is bolstered by the further concern that discretion will breed differential treatment of similar cases. The latter is a concern that officials share, along with the expectation that they must consistently anticipate legal challenges, media scrutiny, and Congressional criticism.

Vague statutes pass the ball to executive agencies, who proceed to drop it nicely by composing detailed regulations to cover every conceivable case, reducing the discretion available to a bare minimum. Regulation is further influenced by the legal restrictions Congress and the courts have imposed, restrictions of a procedural sort that are to ensure that everyone with a legitimate concern can have a say. The elaborate procedures for making and applying rules result in paperwork and delay, and when such procedures are instituted at government command in other organizations, there is further paperwork and delay.

Regulations, like statutes, also allow their creators to demonstrate that they are doing something, too. There is no overwhelming confidence among wise bureaucrats that many of their regulations will induce the desired results, but one cannot always tell the Congress or Ralph Nader that. Once evidence piles up that the costs are excessive and results meager, that unpleasant fact might be confronted, but not before.

Another thing to consider is the fact that to outsiders federal agencies often appear very powerful. But that is not the way it usually looks on the inside, which is why, in enforcement efforts on anti-discrimination regulations, for instance, officials take such a hard-nosed stance, investigate even flimsy complaints, demand all sorts of information, adopt an accusatory tone. The starting assumption of the agency must be that discrimination has occurred and is occurring. Since enforcement focuses on complaints, the agency necessarily assumes an adversarial stance as the agent of the complaining party. Thus the other party must prove its innocence, must prove discrimination did not occur. To do a preliminary investigation to see if the complaint had any merit would be almost collusion with the adversary. Because the accused must prove innocence, the request for huge amounts of information logically follows. The agency will normally lack the personnel and other resources to enforce the regulations in detail throughout the country. Often its ultimate weapon is a cutoff in funds, something extreme and imprecise and sure to bring more skirmishes in court and in Congress. Thus the agency's most useful power is the power to harass, a weapon that can be employed irrespective of the merits of the particular complaint. In fact, complaints are primarily useful as opportunities to exercise that power, to create examples that will help scare others into compliance. Resistance to such harassment is, from an agency's point of view, a move to strip it of one of the most valuable means at its disposal to carry out its responsibilities.

There are other ways in which avoiding risks shapes regulator action. The lawyers involved have a natural tendency to cover all possible contingencies as a defense against possible lawsuits, which is perfectly understandable given the ominous increase in litigation in the United States. Once drafted and printed in the *Federal Register,* regulations are hard to get altered because changes may open the agency to charges of error or incompetence, or to deferring too much to the interests of those to be regulated, particularly when those charges may be made by the forces that pushed for the regulations in the first place and by Congressmen. Risk-avoidance also dictates the gauntlet of sign-offs and clearances that regulations, decisions, even simple communications from one office to another must run, a source of the considerable delays in the government.

The President, too, must live with political and administrative pressures to legislate and regulate. He has to demonstrate that something is being done to fend off the constant political pressures referred to earlier. He has to weigh battling Congress and the bureaucracy to reform the administrative structure against his need for their support to get other important things done. Often he needs to put some distance between himself and the regulatory machinery so that the criticism that inevitably arises does not reflect on him. It is no accident that recent presidents have run on platforms opposing "the mess in Washington."

RECOMMENDATIONS

The following review is a relatively comprehensive list of proposed solutions. They must be examined together because it is clear that we have a Hydra on our hands; multiple reforms must be pressed simultaneously to get even partial relief. Not all reforms are appropriate for every kind of regulation; what works in one place may well make things worse in another. As former President Ford has suggested, we must think in terms of packages of reforms.[14] Proposed reforms that the Business–Higher Education Forum could consider supporting fall into the following categories:

1. *Make officials confront the further efforts of what they plan to do by requiring draft legislation and regulations to include analysis of prospective inflationary impact, costs, and paperwork burdens involved.* Observers regularly assert that those who legislate and regulate with gusto do so in ignorance of the burdens they impose. The House and Senate have requirements of this sort for bills, as does President Carter's Executive Order 12044. Several bills have been introduced that would go further, by having Congress set an overall economic impact level above which the total regulatory effort could not go, mandating cost-benefit analyses of alternative regulatory patterns and requiring selection of the least burdensome one in every case. The Regulatory Reform Act of 1979, S. 262, cosponsored by Senators Ribicoff, Percy, Kennedy, Javits, and others, is perhaps the best case in point and stands the best chance of passage.

14. Gerald Ford, "Seizing the Opportunity," *Regulation*, Jan/Feb 1978, pp. 15–17.

Attractive as all this sounds, the approach is not without drawbacks. It would invite lots of fuzzy figures because there is no agreement on how to define "costs" and to calculate them. The recent Business Roundtable study, for example, is a highly commendable effort at rigorous analysis, but it does illustrate problems in handling definitions, data, costs, and benefits. Just as with the costs of regulation, many of the benefits sought are noneconomic in nature and impossible to measure, making it possible for those to pick the numbers they find congenial, further clouding the murky situation in which the country finds itself.

2. *Make the government pay the costs of compliance.* This action is particularly attractive to higher education institutions, because they cannot readily pass along increased costs to their consumers or take them off as tax deductions. It is used somewhat in the allowances for administrative expenses in student aid programs, and perhaps it would help to extend the practice further. Of course, there is no getting around the difficulty of accurately computing real costs, so the subsidies will inevitably be too much or too little.

However, the real problem lies elsewhere. If the government pays, it will want still more information on what happens to the money and soon it will want more influence over the costs themselves, as amply illustrated by developments in the health care field. The requirement also encourages government to be less sensitive to complaints, on the principle that "they are getting their money, what have they got to complain about."

There are also political difficulties involved. As noted earlier, pressures for regulation often come from people who find cost considerations distasteful or irrelevant, and they will assuredly resist the idea of compensating someone to do the right thing. They will see this as an effort to water down the government's commitments by making them expensive, and to make money out of efforts to ensure their vision of a decent society.

3. *Create a Congressional committee or related entity to review regulatory authorities and determine those that should be curtailed.* Congress has the habit of seizing on a problem, asserting a vague commitment to solve it, and leaving the details to the executive branch. Handed a few vague statements in a statute, bureaucratic spiders spin awesome regulatory webs. It may be in the public interest for Congress to take back much of the authority it has granted to

31

regulate. In addition, one analyst has suggested limiting the length of future regulations to that of the authorizing legislation or relevant portion thereof. Theodore Lowi urges that presidents veto, and courts refuse to enforce, statutes that fail to clearly set forth the problem, the policies to be adopted, and the criteria to be used in devising actions.[15] Another possible action is more use of the "legislative veto" under which Congress would insist that regulations issued by agencies are subject to a veto (by one or both houses).

Congressional propensity for passing legislation that is too detailed does not seem to be the answer either. Trying to get legislation sufficiently clear and precise, with appropriate provision for procedural safeguards to handle the specific cases that will arise, probably cannot be done without detailed and convoluted Congressional instructions. Such instructions will do just as much harm as if they originated with the agencies. Even if it is theoretically possible to write legislation exceedingly clear and concise, who can be optimistic about getting Congress to change its ways?

4. *Require that all regulatory agencies and their regulations lapse after a period of time unless permitted by the Congress to continue.* Lowi has suggested having legislation lapse automatically after ten years to force a periodic reexamination and require a positive decision to let it continue. The essence of numerous "sunset" proposals is that agencies, and their regulations, go out of business unless reviewed and expressly permitted to continue by Congress. A number of states have enacted such legislation, and many bills to foster this have been introduced in Congress. The foremost champions of sunset legislation have been Senators Edmund Muskie and Charles Percy, who have sought to place all major federal programs on an eight-year cycle. Plans for program reform and continuation would be submitted by the President, but if Congress chose not to act, the programs would be shut down, with their vital functions transferred to other agencies.

Sunset legislation is one of those ideas that appears sound until one remembers that the government would have to carry it out. All programs have clients who will mightily resist shutting down "their" agencies. All federal programs exist because they have found a home in Congress, and the committees will vigorously resist eliminating "their" programs. All will join hands in perfunctory reviews of

15. See Lowi, loc. cit., and Hugh Latimer, "A Case of Runaway Regulation, Premerger Notification," *Regulation,* May/June 1979, pp. 46–52.

agencies and programs and in logrolling to trade saving one program for saving another. Presidents will logroll, too, treating this as another new tool for trying to manage Congress. Finally, it will be impossible for Congress to consider huge batches of programs carefully within a short time span. Either the cycle will have to be stretched or the Congress will likely breeze through it.[16] Common Cause has recognized some of these difficulties, which is why it argues that sunset reforms must include a reform of the committee system in Congress, including rotation of members among the various committees.

5. *Consider alternatives to regulation.* Regulation is costly and time consuming and breeds paperwork. Why not search for alternative ways to handle areas targeted for regulation? Critics charge that legislators, especially lawyers, reflexively think in terms of law, while bureaucrats instinctively seek to write rules and gather reports. Neither group apparently seriously considers alternatives.

One alternative frequently suggested is to have the government develop broad standards or levels of performance but not specify how compliance is to be attained. For instance, OSHA could set maximum tolerable accident rates for industries but let firms decide how best to achieve those rates. Then firms would be able to pick the most comfortable, least costly, or most efficient way to comply. This approach would avoid setting detailed rules in Washington that inevitably are not quite right in Georgia.

Another alternative is better use of self-regulation. There is a good deal of this already in some industries and in many professions, including the accreditation process in higher education. But self-regulation is haphazard, often too protective of the industry or profession involved, and not designed to meet the problems the government wants solved. There is no inherent reason why this must be so. Too often the choice is between extensive government regulation and the free market; we have not seen these as the end points on a continuum and have used little creativity or imagination to fill the spaces in between. For example, the government might indicate its objectives but let the affected industries and other sectors develop, and even enforce, the necessary regulations. Perhaps the government can be induced to design regulations that are replaced by self-regulation beyond a certain point, with the government settling for performance

16. Robert Behn, "The False Dawn of the Sunset Laws," *The Public Interest*, No. 49 (Fall 1977), pp. 103–118.

standards from then on. The government would be using regulations to get things moving in the right direction, after which its intrusion could be reduced in favor of letting things continue on their own.

Recently, just the threat that there could be regulation was enough to get various higher education associations to endorse principles on recruiting and admissions and on refunding fees to students who leave; perhaps this will settle the matter with no further intervention by the Office of Education. Maybe the government would do better to indicate intentions more and regulate less.

Further along this road is the use of incentives rather than regulations. The government might offer subsidies to induce desired behavior. Alternatives here include tax breaks, tax credits, and direct financial support for the costs of compliance, particularly when new technology is involved. A troublesome point is the money. The most attractive method for providing incentives, then, is to deregulate, allowing market forces to play a larger role, because the new economic incentives for firms need not come at government expense. The government could go further by using fines and taxes to penalize, for example, firms that pollute excessively or those that tolerate high accident rates, thereby providing economic incentives to discontinue such behavior.

Intellectually, economists favor use of markets, finding them to be efficient, even-handed, nonintrusive, and highly rational devices for coordination of human behavior.[17] In studies of regulated industries some economists have concluded that government intervention stifles competition and that this leads to excessively high prices, inefficient industries, and insufficient innovation, on top of the delays, red tape, and costs associated with regulation itself.[18] Substantial deregulation is their antidote, and it has begun to occur in a few industries and to be given serious consideration for others.

Charles Schultze would have us use market-type incentives in place of many kinds of "command and control" regulations. One of his favorite examples is pollution. How does the government tackle the

17. A most important book on the whole subject of markets and their relationship to political systems is Charles Lindblom, *Politics and Markets* (New York: Basic Books, 1977).

18. See the many studies in *Study on Federal Regulation, Committee on Governmental Affairs, United States Senate, Appendix to Volume VI, Framework For Regulation* (Washington: Government Printing Office, 1978); and some of the articles in *Regulating Business: The Search For An Optimum* (San Francisco: Institute For Contemporary Studies, 1978).

thousands upon thousands of individual sources of pollution by means of regulations specifying what is to be done that will cover each and every instance? The answer is it cannot, at least not without creating a bureaucratic nightmare. Suppose it simply taxed pollution? Then polluters would have an incentive to cut back on their harmful emissions, to research ways to avoid pollution, and to regulate themselves.

Performance standards and market incentives are certainly attractive for dealing with some kinds of regulatory problems. They will not work everywhere, but in many cases they promise substantial benefits. There are some drawbacks to consider, however. In the Soviet Union the government sets output targets and performance standards all the time as its way of running the entire economy. The results are not reassuring. Setting the targets for shoes in terms of the amount of leather used leads to production of big leather shoes wastefully made. Setting the targets for shoes in numbers of shoes means lots of very small shoes cheaply made (and almost no big ones). Setting the targets in terms of so many shoes of each kind and each size means production is not responsive to whether or not anyone will buy them. Setting output targets by quarter leads to a mad scramble at the end of each quarter to meet the plan, by overworking the machines, sacrificing quality, putting workers on expensive overtime, all the penalties of what Russians call "rush work." In other words, performance standards may evoke compliance through unsatisfactory methods, which is why regulations so specify not only objectives but the ways they are to be achieved.

Schultze himself has pointed to problems with respect to the greater use of market incentives. Markets often have the effect of benefiting some people at the expense of others, so increased use of markets would produce some "losers." Our political system is poorly designed for deliberately creating losers; they will object and their objections will have political effect. The result is apt to be renewed tampering with the market. Schultze would have us pay more attention to compensation of losers when market forces are employed, so as to reduce the complaints. He also notes that, to a Congressman, markets avoid the endless bureaucratic processing of specific cases and thus offer little opportunity to intervene and be of service to aggrieved constituents. This drawback makes market solutions less attractive and there is no easy way around this political difficulty.

A still larger problem, says Schultze, is that getting the government to take up a major social problem entails a long slow process of generating a sufficient consensus, in the society and in the government. Once that finally appears, everyone wants action at once, a set of directives and a program, not some tinkering with market incentives, the effects of which will not be apparent for years. Schultze has faith that we are mature enough as a society to settle for the longer range solution when we have the alternatives properly explained, but displays concern that he has no stronger answer for this problem.

There are other difficulties Schultze does not consider. We would have to rely on the tax system still more, and we do not normally consider it virtuous when it comes to red tape. How will we determine the acceptable levels of effluents? We will need more paperwork and investigations. What are the actual outputs so we know how much to charge? More inspectors, reports, disputes, appeals, lawsuits, and so on. Another problem, pointed out before, is that many people who want regulations want to punish evil and stamp out harm; they don't want to put the problem in a cost-benefit, market framework. Schultze notes with dismay that some major statutes expressly require that the agency involved ignore economic considerations in arriving at standards and deadlines. Some people do not like markets for the subjects at hand, do not like getting results via a market mechanism, do not like motivating people in that way. Others will object that the true costs are simply going to be passed on to the consumer, whether firms comply or not, or that firms will arrange to "cook" the market or the government incentives so that they benefit handsomely. People who think like economists want everyone to consider the trade-offs and opportunity costs involved in doing anything, including good works. People seeking regulation often see trade-offs as an excuse for not doing what ought to be done. That is the difference between seeing trade-offs as normal, as economists do, and deplorable, as regulators often do. The point here is that there are no simple solutions. Distortions in markets can come from many sources. The challenge is to seek broad consensus in American society on meshing social goals with efficient markets in a manner as intelligent and realistic as possible.

6. *Build a better government.* Maybe the real solution is to get the government to be efficient and well organized. This has particular appeal to people in the government. It implies they are doing important and valuable things, just not doing them well enough. Hence

this is the kind of solution that executive orders, the Office of Management and Budget, the Federal Paperwork Commission, and various other governmental reform efforts always emphasize.

There are endless ways the government could stand improvement. Here are the most frequently proposed reforms or ones recently adopted. Everyone agrees that the responsibilities of agencies and their regulations too often overlap, which produces duplication in the information they seek and confusing differences in the standards they impose. It would be helpful to diminish this, such as by designating a lead agency in a particular matter (like affirmative action or protection of human subjects) and requiring all other agencies involved to imitate its requirements. This approach has only been taken occasionally. Of course, the goal could also be reached by eliminating the competing agencies and programs, enthusiasm for which in the government is restrained.

Agency practices can be improved, of course. President Carter has ordered that regulations be written in plain English, and it has been suggested by others that the *Federal Register* be empowered to refuse to print poorly written materials. There are periodic calls for the appointment of better people to manage regulatory agencies, and to require that agency heads give personal attention to improving the regulations issued in their names. The Federal Paperwork Commission proposed that each agency develop a comprehensive plan as to the information it really needs, and when, and why, and some steps in this direction have been taken. Everyone thinks regulations could be briefer and simpler than at present. Delays in agency decisions and actions often result from what critics regard as excessively formal (quasi-judicial) hearing procedures and enforcement actions, too many appeal processes, and too many layers of required reviews and clearances. The Paperwork Commission suggested that each agency name a high-level official as contact person on paperwork problems, someone with real authority to cut through red tape and deal with complaints. A popular proposal is that agencies undertake regular reviews of required reports, standard forms, and regulations in order to weed out unnecessary, duplicative, and unwieldy ones.

The agencies would be more likely to do these things if subjected to more central direction of regulatory activities. Executive orders in the past two administrations as well as a Carter bill now before Congress have been designed to do this. The general thrust is to

37

strengthen the hand of OMB in clearing forms (tightening enforcement of the Federal Reports Act, for instance), requiring agencies to submit plans for information and regulation, and setting general guidelines for all agencies. To assist in this process, the administration has created a Federal Information Locator System, so agencies can find out what the government already knows and not request the information again, a Regulatory Council which publishes a semi-annual calendar of forthcoming regulations, and a Regulatory Analysis Review Group, in which high-level officials are supposed to review 15–20 major regulations annually. The Paperwork Commission concluded that all such work should be consolidated in a cabinet Department of Administration.

Generally, those functions properly the responsibility of the government need better management. To this end, the powers of Office of Management and Budget need to be given a new, stronger mandate that would require a program of management improvement of all government agencies and evidence of annual progress.

7. *Make government accessible.* Many of the mistakes made by government officials are often said to result from ignorance about how the country works, from the insularity of the Washington bureaucracy, and from the bureaucrat's tendency to respond too much to his own interests. The solution is to inject more participation by outsiders into the regulatory process. Proposed reforms generally concentrate on getting more discussion and bargaining between agencies and those they regulate, particularly while regulations and forms are still in the draft stage. The practice of seeking comments on a published draft is seen as unsatisfactory because drafts often seem set in stone. Agencies might be required to allow a longer time for receiving comments. They could be asked to seek comments on the dates regulations are to take effect, not just on what they will require.

THINKING ABOUT REFORM

How can leaders in business and higher education best promote regulatory reform? Many of the "large" problems described above can be eased if a concerted effort is made to advocate and implement some or all of the preceding suggestions. The "particularly significant" problem will never go away, but it too will yield to the right strategy for reform. Here are some guidelines for thinking about reform.

On the "large" problems, the primary lesson of the general survey and analysis in this paper is that, realistically, we can expect to do no better than reform at the margins; improvement will come in the form of moderate reductions in the degree of irritation, but not the elimination of it.[19] Expectations need to be set accordingly.

Next, reform is most readily attained when those who complain can define their specific objections, point out the particular things they want changed, and *offer a detailed solution*. As Herbert Kaufman has observed:

> The [American] system responds to pointed demands for specific actions, not to grand visions or all-embracing lamentations . . . railing against all red tape or advocating some panacea that will purportedly dispose of it once and for all avails nothing; an attack on a particular agency or on a designated tax or application form or on a specific requirement long since out of date is much more likely to get results.[20]

Because several solutions are typically needed for each particular problem and because each industry, institution, and part of society has its specific difficulties with regulation, packages of reforms must be considered, with each package tailored to the needs of the particular industry or sector of society that is willing to fight for it. It is proposed here that business and higher education join in a political coalition to confront regulation, even though it should be fully understood that such a coalition cannot be put together to fight the battles of each industry or sector of higher education. Entities would neither share the same interests and perspectives nor have the same priorities or solutions in mind. In the end, the coalition would fail to endorse sufficiently specific remedies to meet the peculiar needs of each of its members. Thus, joining forces is a supplement, not a substitute, for continuing efforts to have individual grievances alleviated.

A broad coalition, built around a stronger business–higher education relationship in general, could sustain a general political pressure for reform and to build on the relatively favorable climate between business and higher education leaders that has emerged in the past few years. Such a coalition could make judicious use of the usual mechanisms of political influence. Efforts to educate Congress and the public on the regulatory process and its effects should be coordinated and strengthened. The Business–Higher Education Forum could consider establishing a standing committee of distinguished citizens to oversee political and educational efforts and to report

19. The best discussion of why this is so is Herbert Kaufman, *Red Tape, Its Origins, Uses, and Abuses* (Washington: The Brookings Institution, 1977).
20. Ibid., pp. 87–88.

periodically on the progress, or lack of it, being made. The coalition could also provide a framework for the exchange of ideas and sharing of experiences, on how to live with certain types of regulation or on proper tactics for seeking changes. One or more conferences for this purpose could be sponsored, and circulation of valuable studies or background information could be promoted. Research on aspects of the problem could be commissioned and promoted.

The coalition could also consider endorsing some of the reforms reviewed earlier in this paper, with due attention to the attendant difficulties and drawbacks. A good candidate is the sunset legislation now before Congress; prospects for passage appear favorable in the near future. Sunset legislation will have little effect if someone does not hold Congress accountable, however, and assist in generating necessary information about the impact of regulation, during the cycle of program review. Also, the coalition might express strong support for the general principles of relying more on market incentives, performance standards, and self-regulation.

The coalition would also be able to endorse administrative reforms. Some have already been mentioned, but there are other possibilities. In the White House, a Council of Regulatory Advisors or an Office of Regulatory Ombudsman might be established as a manifestation of every recent president's expressed interest in gaining control over regulatory excesses. Or there could be an Office of Regulatory Assessment, a National Regulatory Board, or even, though this is the least likely, the Department of Administration advocated by the Federal Paperwork Commission.

On the "particularly significant" problem there are only a few possible solutions. One would be to have a lot less government, presumably by asking the government to do a lot less. One analyst with considerable experience in the shortcomings of government concludes that

> . . . government ought not to do many of the things liberal reform has traditionally asked of it; and even when, in some abstract sense, government does pursue appropriate goals, it is not very suited to achieving them. . . . Government is probably less sensible and less reliable than liberal reformers have been willing to admit. . . . It is . . . essential to become more modest in our demands on, and expectations of, the institutions of representative government.[21]

21. Eugene Bardach, *The Implementation Game: What Happens After A Bill Becomes A Law* (Cambridge: MIT Press, 1977), p. 283.

However desirable less government might be, it seems more likely that Americans are going to continue to rely on the government for a great many things. That means we will have to put up with the way it works. It is as it is, because of our history, our political system, and our political traditions. Total reform would have to overcome all those things, which is impossible, and indeed undesirable. Americans will have to go on dragging the red tape equivalent of Morley's chains, at best snipping off a link here or there.

So there is need to come to terms with the nature of modern life in our society with the help of a new conception of the best ordering of things, a conception in which government is an unavoidable partner. The government will continue to be intrusive and bureaucratic; it will help a good deal but at a price. Dreams of operating in self-regulating markets or as institutions of fully autonomous professionals, with government merely a crude excrescence on what really matters, must be set aside. It is within this new framework that we must press for a more satisfactory relationship with the government.

GETTING RECOMMENDATIONS ACCEPTED

Recommendations generated by this analysis will require major changes in governmental outlook and practice. Such changes will not happen unless the voting public wants and demands it, and unless a general policy on regulation is established. The generation of consensus among the voting public can be built through the establishment of the coalition just described and wide publication of this statement and other analyses of regulatory problems. The general policy on regulation should be based on the following principles.[22]

1. It shall be the firm policy of the government to see that the freedom of action and self-management of private-sector organizations and institutions is not weakened by intrusion of federal laws and regulations.
2. To that end, there must be a clear assertion in every instance, by the Congress or a regulatory agency, that a proposed statute or

22. An alternative set of three "criteria" for screening requests for regulation, criteria too narrow to deal with the fundamental issue of federal intrusion, can be found in *Redefining Government's Role in the Market System,* a Statement by the Research and Policy Committee of the Committee for Economic Development (New York: Committee for Economic Development, 1979), pp. 22–23.

set of regulations that will reduce the autonomy and freedom of action of some portion of the private sector:

   a. will do so in pursuit of objectives that have been judged to be sufficiently important to make the intrusion necessary and valid; and

   b. will be subject to periodic review on these grounds, and will be erased upon evidence that the results are insufficient to justify continued intrusion or that the intrusion is too severe.

3. Intrusion will be considered significant when:

   a. it requires a major shift in institutional/organizational priorities;

   b. it requires elimination or major alteration of significant outputs, practices, or processes; and

   c. it requires an increase in the organization/institution budget for purposes of compliance of a percentage amount reasonable for each industry or category of institutions.

4. Statutes and regulations will reflect consideration of alternative available means to achieve their objectives, with priority given to selection of the least intrusive.

5. All regulations issued by executive agencies must be explicitly authorized by statute or clearly in keeping with Congressional intent.

6. All regulations and the corresponding statutes must be reviewed at least once every ten years to assure that they remain in conformity with these principles.

7. Agencies shall issue periodic reports on the degree to which they uphold and comply with these principles in their regulations and activities, shall solicit public comments on these reports, and shall issue summaries and analyses of these comments.

These principles, or similar ones, should be strongly recommended to the President with the goal of having them issued as part of an executive order. They should be embodied in draft legislation presented to the Congress. They should be proposed for inclusion in the platforms of both parties for the upcoming election year. The principles are broad, but the presumption would be that regulation can and should be contained. The idea is to accept the need for regulation while prescribing some fundamental limits beyond which it should not cross. Then the burden of proof for expanding the regulatory complex, particularly when the intrusion will be glaring, will be placed on those proposing such steps.

These are not undue restrictions. Elements of them can be found in many past and present efforts at reform within the government. They are not rigid and fix no permanent lines. Yet they clearly express a *general policy on regulation.* This would supply central direction to the efforts of elected and bureaucratic officials in the general area of regulation. That would be a favorable development.

Policies to Promote Productivity Growth

JOHN W. KENDRICK

THERE IS NOW BROAD PUBLIC RECOGNITION OF THE FACT THAT THE growth of productivity—here defined as output per hour of labor—has been slowing down in the United States since the mid-1960s. It is generally understood that the productivity slowdown has been associated with accelerating inflation, an absence of increases in real average weekly or annual labor compensation, depreciation of the dollar, and balance of trade and payments difficulties (see Table 1). For the past few years, congressional committees have been holding hearings on productivity and related problems, and in its 1979 annual and mid-year reports, the Joint Economic Committee (JEC) has strongly advised the desirability of effective legislation to stimulate investment and renewed productivity growth as a means of reducing inflation, raising real incomes, and helping solve international economic problems.[1] It appears likely that tax and other legislation will be passed in 1980 to stimulate investment and aggregate demand, as well as to spur productivity and increase supply capabilities.

The heart of this paper lies in the presentation and discussion of the policy options available to promote productivity growth, organized in terms of eight major groups of causal forces. Some of the policy measures are alternatives; most are complementary. Some would cost little or nothing, or even reduce costs (e.g., the elimination of unproductive regulations); the real cost of most would depend on the size of the programs or tax cuts approved. In some cases, analyses of the relative effectiveness of alternative policies—mainly those to stimulate investment—are examined. More policy studies

1. *The 1979 Joint Economic Report*, Report of the Joint Economic Committee, Congress of the United States, on the 1979 Economic Report of the President, together with supplementary and additional views (Washington: U.S. Government Printing Office, 1979.)

TABLE 1: *Average Annual Percentage Rates of Change in Productivity and Related Variables, 1948–78, by Three Subperiods*

Productivity and Related Variables	1948–66	1966–73	1973–78
U.S. business economy			
Total factor productivity	2.8	1.6	0.8
Real product per labor hour	3.4	2.1	1.1
U.S. nonagricultural business			
Real product per hour	2.8	1.9	1.0
Real average weekly earnings	2.2	1.6	−0.9
Real average hourly earnings	2.4	1.6	−0.1
Nominal average hourly earnings	5.2	6.9	9.0
Labor costs per unit of output	1.8	4.7	7.8
Average prices	1.8	4.3	7.5

Source: Based on estimates from the Bureau of Labor Statistics, U.S. Department of Labor, except for total factor productivity estimates from John W. Kendrick and Elliot Grossman, *Productivity in the United States: Trends and Cycles* (Baltimore: Johns Hopkins University Press, 1979).

are needed, but the present assemblage and discussion of a wide variety of options will be helpful to various groups in deciding which policy measures they can support, and to the executive and legislative branches of the federal government in formulating a balanced program to reverse the productivity slowdown. As the mid-year (August 1979) report of the Joint Economic Committee of Congress states:

> America's dismal productivity performance is an important cause of the nation's stagflation . . . the solution lies in the adoption of longer-run policies aimed at expanding the supply of the economy; that is, at expanding the nation's productive potential in a manner that raises dramatically the growth of American productivity.[2]

THE ROLES OF BUSINESS AND HIGHER EDUCATION

It is appropriate that the Business–Higher Education Forum should have selected the enhancement of productivity growth as an area of mutual concern and possible joint action. The functions of both sec-

2. Midyear Report and Staff Study of the Joint Economic Committee, Congress of the United States, "Outlook 1980's" (August 1979), p. 6.

John W. Kendrick is professor of economics at George Washington University and former chief economist, U.S. Department of Commerce.

The opinions and recommendations in this paper are those of the author and are not intended to represent the official policy or endorsement of the Business–Higher Education Forum or the American Council on Education.

tors are centrally related to productivity, and the leaders of business and of education can play a more important role in accelerating productivity growth than is possible for any other sector, leaving aside for the moment the federal government, which establishes the legal and institutional framework within which the private sectors operate. Indeed, most of the recommendations in this paper relate to federal policies that would stimulate the various economic sectors to do a better job in performing their productivity-enhancing functions. The achievement of a stronger and a steadier rate of growth of productivity and of real income and product would, of course, benefit all sectors, including business and education.

Business

The business role in increasing productivity is very direct: management must operate efficiently in order to realize adequate rates of return on investment. But the unique entrepreneurial function is to innovate—to develop new products and processes and to invest in new capital facilities to produce the new products and to implement the cost-reducing technologies. For many firms, this function involves substantial investments in research and development, an alert purchasing policy that takes advantage of new equipment or other producers' goods, and organizational changes that would reduce costs and thus increase productivity. It also means providing training and retraining of workers to operate the new plants and equipment. In a dynamic economy, it means staying alert to current and projected marketing opportunities and being flexibile in shifting resources and altering combinations of factor inputs to minimize costs and to maximize net income. In our type of economy, rates of return temporarily in excess of the opportunity cost of capital are considered to be a socially desirable incentive and reward for successful innovation. But a firm must continue to stay ahead of its competitors technologically in order to continue to be able to earn above-average profits.

Many of the recommendations in this paper are for tax reforms and other measures to create a favorable investment climate and provide rates of return on business outlays for research and development (R&D) and new capital goods that are adequate to stimulate stronger increases in investment, and thus in productivity, than in the past decade. Improving the investment climate also involves removing disincentives and impediments to technological progress, such as excessive or misdirected regulations.

As the Administration and Congress gradually formulate policy measures to stimulate investment and productivity, businessmen and their representatives must have an input into the process. Several reports of the industry subcommittees of the Domestic Policy Review Committee on Industrial Innovation,[3] which are referred to below, stressed the desirability of government agencies shifting emphasis from an adversarial stance vis-à-vis business to a more cooperative relationship. Certainly, consultations with business leaders in formulating policies to revise tax laws, reform regulatory procedures and rules, and otherwise improve the investment environment are essential, as will be a positive business response.

Higher education

The role of higher education in productivity advance is not as immediate as that of business, but it is fundamental in that the educational system is largely responsible for transmitting and enhancing the body of knowledge through the generations. It is mainly through educational processes that the nonmaterial investments in human beings are made that prepare them for productive roles in the economy and the broader society; and increases in the quantity and quality of human investments are considered to be a major element in increasing productivity. More specifically, institutions of higher education prepare the scientists, engineers, and business administrators who make the inventions, develop them for commercial use, and make the decisions to invest in the new processes, plants, and equipment. A coordinate function of the higher education system is to perform basic research that advances scientific knowledge, which feeds into applied R&D, and in turn is benefited by it. To some extent, universities and other nonprofit institutions become involved in applied R&D,

3. The Draft Reports of the Advisory Subcommittees were issued in late December 1978 by the National Technical Information Service, U.S. Department of Commerce, under the following titles and numbers:
Patent Policy, PB 290403
Information Policy, PB 290404
Environmental, Health, and Safety Regulations, PB 290405
Direct Federal Support of Research Development, PB 290407
Regulation of Industry Structures and Competition, PB 290409
Economic and Trade Policy, PB 290415
Federal Procurement Policy, PB 290417

in part as a means of training students for this function, which makes them more directly relevant to productivity growth. Research in the medical and health area and health education also help increase the quality and productivity of human capital.

More broadly, the educational system as a whole educates and prepares future members of the labor force to operate the increasingly complex technology of industry, although specific training is generally performed within the business sector in special courses or on the job. Indirectly, the education system contributes to resource mobility, because more highly educated workers are generally more mobile. Although the effort and efficiency with which workers perform their duties are a responsibility of management, the values and attitudes of members of the labor forces are an important background element that is influenced by their educational experience. Understanding of the economic system generally and of the role of productivity in the realization of individual, business, and social goals, and a broader comprehension of our political and social institutions, conduce to more effective participation in economic and other functions of the society. Although far from realization, this goal of preparing young people for effective and productive living remains a major challenge to education.

Through social and economic analysis and projections of trends, the academic community contributes background studies required by business for long-range planning, which facilitates resource reallocations in response to anticipated shifts in demand and supply and other dynamic economic and social forces. Likewise, objective academic studies are helpful to governments in trying to adapt laws and regulations to changing conditions, and to make them a more effective framework for eliciting the creative and productive energies of the private sectors through socially beneficial channels. For example, the many analytical studies of the sources of increases in productivity, which were drawn upon in this paper as background for presenting a menu of policy options, should be helpful to legislators in deciding on specific, feasible measures to attain that goal.

Well-researched, analytically sound, and objective studies may get nowhere, however, unless influential constituencies apply persuasion to legislators to act on the recommendations that flow from the studies. It is encouraging that the Business–Higher Education Forum is seeking common ground with respect to policies to promote productivity growth that would be consistent with the best interests of both groups. In the presentation and discussion of the policy options in this paper, no attempt is made to single out those options that may appeal most to both. But a concluding section highlights the kinds of policies that would seem to have the most attraction.

There can be no doubt that the achievement of a stronger and steadier rate of growth in productivity and in real income and product will be of benefit to business, to education, and indeed to every part of the economy. A rising real income per capita, made possible by rising productivity, is a near-universal objective of this and most other societies, and one that makes the attainment of other objectives more feasible. And, as Professor Dunlop pointed out in his concluding address to the first Forum in January 1979, both business and education have a deeper interest in the good health and survival of our type of economic system, to which productivity growth importantly contributes. The dispersion of economic and political power that goes with a system of private property and economic freedom is a bulwark protecting civil liberties and academic freedom. But our economic and academic freedoms carry with them responsibilities to act in accordance with the common good. This includes cooperation in the solution of pressing economic problems, to which a resumption of vigorous productivity growth is a key.

CAUSAL FACTORS UNDERLYING PRODUCTIVITY GROWTH

Formulating policies to promote productivity requires an understanding of the chief sets of causal forces behind the growth of productivity. This section explains the analytical framework in which the recommendations are presented, with reference to the schema shown in Table 2. The table contains rates of change in output (real product), inputs (labor, capital, and total), and productivity for the U.S. domestic business economy over the three subperiods 1948–66, 1966–73, and 1973–78. It also shows the estimated percentage point contributions of eight groups and selected subgroups of causal factors to the rate of change in real product per labor hour. The latter variable may be calculated either as the average annual percentage rate of change between the boundary years of the ratio of real product to labor hours or as the difference between the rates of change in real product and in labor-hour input. The latter formulation is why pro-

TABLE 2: *Sources of Growth in Real Gross Product, Average Annual Percentage Rates of Change, U.S. Domestic Business Economy Percentage Points, Selected Subperiods, 1948–1978*

Sources	1948–66	1966–73	1973–78
Real Gross Product	3.9	3.5	2.4
Factor Input—Total	1.1	1.9	1.6
Labor	0.4	1.4	1.3
Capital	2.8	3.3	2.3
Real Product Per Unit of Labor	3.5	2.1	1.1
Capital/Labor Substitution	0.7	0.5	0.3
Total Factor Productivity	2.8	1.6	0.8
Sources of Total Factor Productivity Growth: (Percentage Point Contribution)			
Advances in Knowledge	1.4	1.1	0.8
R&D Stock	0.85	0.75	0.6
Informal	0.3	0.25	0.2
Rate of Diffusion	0.25	0.1	—
Changes in Labor Quality	0.6	0.4	0.7
Education & Training	0.6	0.7	0.8
Health	0.1	0.1	0.1
Age/Sex Composition	−0.1	−0.4	−0.2
Changes in Quality of Land	—	−0.1	−0.2
Resource Reallocations	0.8	0.7	0.3
Labor	0.4	0.2	0.1
Capital	0.4	0.5	0.2
Volume Changes	0.4	0.2	−0.1
Economics of Scale	0.4	0.3	0.2
Intensity of Demand	—	−0.1	−0.3
Net Government Impact	—	−0.1	−0.3
Services to Business	0.1	0.1	0.1
Regulations	−0.1	−0.2	−0.4
Actual/Potential Efficiency, and n.e.c.°	−0.4	−0.6	−0.4

° n.e.c. = not elsewhere classified

Source: John W. Kendrick, based in part on estimates by Edward F. Denison, *Accounting for United States Economic Growth, 1948–1969* (Brookings, 1974).

ductivity change is sometimes called the "residual"—that part of the change in output not explained by the change in input.

Ever since the 1950s, a number of economists have been trying to analyze and explain the residual, and thus the causes of productivity change. The pioneering work of Edward F. Denison in "growth accounting" has been particularly useful.[4] The schema used in Table 1 and many of the estimates are based largely on his approach, with

4. Edward F. Denison, *Accounting for United States Economic Growth, 1948–1969* (Washington: The Brookings Institution, 1974).

some rearrangements, elaborations, and additions, as described else-where.[5] Note that the estimates are subject to varying margins of error, some more firmly based than others, but are useful for indicating general orders of magnitude. In any case, the chief use of the schema is for organizing the subsequent discussion of policy options.

A portion of the residual can be explained by the growth of capital (including developed natural resources, as well as man-made capital goods—structures, equipment, and inventory stocks) per unit of labor input. This factor is sometimes called "capital/labor substitution" and is obtained by weighting (multiplying) the rate of growth of real capital per unit of labor by the capital share of gross national income, which is about one-third in recent years. As shown in the table, this factor accounted for 20 percent of the growth of labor productivity during the period 1948–66 and a bit more in subsequent subperiods. The capital and labor inputs are measured without adjustment for changes in their average quantity or efficiency, which are taken account of in other categories of causal forces. The table also shows that capital/labor substitution is the reconciliation item between changes in labor productivity and in "total factor productivity" (TFP), which is the ratio of real product to total factor input—a weighted average of labor and capital inputs.[6] TFP is really a better measure of *net* savings in the tangible factor inputs per unit of output, and thus the increase in productive efficiency generally, than is the output-per-hour ratio, which is affected by changes in input-mix (substitutions) as well as by efficiency changes. But the present official productivity estimates of the Bureau of Labor Statistics (BLS) are confined to the better-known, conventional output-per-hour ratios, so the discussion of causes begins at that point. Denison and the present writer both use the TFP approach, and recently a Panel on Productivity Concepts and Measures, established by the National Academy of Sciences, has recommended that BLS should experiment

5. See *Reaching a Higher Standard of Living* (New York: The New York Stock Exchange, Office of Economic Research, January 1979), Appendix III; and John W. Kendrick, "Productivity Trends and the Recent Slowdown: Historical Perspective, Causal Factors, and Policy Options," in William Fellner, ed., *Contemporary Economic Problems, 1979* (Washington: American Enterprise Institute, 1979), Table 4.

6. For a more extensive discussion of productivity concepts and measures, see the survey of the field by John W. Kendrick, *Understanding Productivity, An Introduction to the Dynamics of Productivity Change* (Baltimore: The Johns Hopkins University Press, 1977).

with multifactor productivity measures, as well as devote more resources to the estimation and analysis of causal factors.[7]

Of the seven groups of causes of TFP growth, by far the most important is advances in technological knowledge as applied to the productive processes through innovations. These advances include the innovations resulting from informal as well as formal research and development programs, as well as the speed with which innovations are diffused throughout the industries of the economy in which they are applicable. In recognition of the importance of technological progress, and of investment in new capital goods in which much of the technological advance is embodied, almost half the recommendations relate to these areas.

The other six factors are (1) changes in the quality of labor as a result of outlays for education, training, health and safety, and changes in the composition of the labor force and employment; (2) changes in the average quality of utilized land and other natural resources; (3) resource reallocations, reflecting the mobility of labor and capital; (4) changes in the volume of production, both secular and cyclical; (5) the positive and negative impacts of governmental interventions in the economy not reflected in the previous categories; and (6) changes in the ratio of actual efficiency under given technologies, and other forces not elsewhere classified (n.e.c.). The forces not elsewhere classified are composed of changes in values, attitudes, and institutions, the effects of which are not captured in the other categories.

By subtracting column three from column one in the table, the contributions of each of the eight sets of causal forces to the 2.4 percent decline in the rate of growth of output per hour between 1948–66 and 1973–78 can be quantified. Five groups of forces each accounted for about one-fifth of the slowdown:

1. a lower rate of capital/labor substitution;
2. slower advances in applied technological knowledge;
3. less favorable effects of interindustry resource shifts;
4. slower economic growth, and a lower rate of utilization of capacity in 1978 than in 1973; and
5. more adverse effects of governmental regulations plus declining average quality of natural resources.

7. See Report of the Panel on Productivity Concepts and Measures (Washington: National Academy of Sciences, Committee on National Statistics, 1979).

Changes in the average quality and efficiency of labor and the n.e.c. factors do not appear to have contributed to the slowdown, although the latter variable had a negative influence in both subperiods. Obviously, positive policies in these areas, as well as policies designed to reverse the drop in the contributions of the other variables, could help improve productivity performance.

Some productivity specialists, including the present writer, believe that even without special policies, productivity growth is likely to be a bit better in the 1980s than it was in the 1970s. Even without a higher investment rate, the projected slowing in the growth of the labor force will mean a correspondingly higher rate of increase in capital per worker. As the youthful bulge in the labor force passes into the middle years, productivity growth will no longer be depressed by the lesser experience of this cohort. Unless new major regulations are imposed, the cost increases required by the present ones should be somewhat less in the 1980s than in the past decade. And if economic growth is stronger than the low 2.8-percent-a-year average increase in real GNP in the past decade, and if cyclical instability is less, this will also be a plus.

But to achieve a significant increase in productivity advance, back up near the rates achieved in the first two decades after World War II, will require a program combining a number of the major types of policy initiatives. One advantage of the comprehensive framework used in this paper and the presentation of a relatively large number of policy proposals (some alternatives and others complementary) is that the interrelationships and common features of the proposals may be observed. The proposals that would tend to bring a convergence of the interests of various sectors and groups of the economy, as well as proposals that would tend to produce a divergence, may also be noted.

Ideally, it would be desirable to have studies done of the relative costs and effectiveness of the various policy alternatives. Some studies are available, but much more policy research is needed. In the meantime, this broad survey of policy options for promoting productivity growth will be of use to various groups in deciding which measures they can support, and to policy advisers and decision makers in formulating a program to reverse the productivity slowdown of recent years. There is no doubt that the time is ripe for such a program and that it will contribute to the solution of other pressing economic problems.

SETS OF POLICY OPTIONS

This section describes the various policy measures and recommendation corresponding to the major groups of causes of productivity growth.

Stimulating business investment and saving

A more vigorous expansion of saving and investment will be needed to accelerate the increase in real capital per unit of labor input, and thus increase the rate of diffusion of innovations through a decline in the average age of plants and equipment. The need is recognized in the 1979 Annual Report of the Council of Economic Advisers (pp. 130–131):

> If the investment needed to reach our economic goals in 1983 is to be realized, policy actions are required that will strengthen investment incentives and reduce investment costs and risks. Tax policy is one instrument that can encourage investment by lowering the rental cost of capital, or raising its after-tax returns. Over the longer term, opportunities for further general tax reduction will emerge. As they do, reductions carefully designed to strengthen incentives for business investment should be given high priority.[8]

This viewpoint was reinforced by the Joint Economic Committee (JEC) in its 1979 Report, Recommendation No. 6: "From a longer run perspective, we need improved incentives to foster savings and investment and job creation."[9] In its midyear report, the JEC was even more positive: "In our view, it is possible to enhance dramatically our potential GNP growth prospects in the coming decade with a carefully designed program aimed at promoting capital investment and upgrading worker skills."[10]

Incentives for increased saving and investment are linked in this section for several reasons. In an accounting sense, the two are equal. Policies to stimulate investment also increase saving, in real terms, if the economy is operating at less than capacity, because increases in investment cause increases in income through the multiplier effect, and increased income generates increased saving as well as consumption. Further, if measures to stimulate investment work by increasing

---

8. *Economic Report of the President,* transmitted to the Congress, on January 1979, together with the Annual Report of the Council of Economic Advisers (Washington: U.S. Government Printing Office, 1979), pp. 130–131.
9. 1979 JEC Report, p. 21.
10. JEC Midyear Report (Summary, August 1979), p. 9.

the after-tax return, increased saving results, because dividend increases lag the profit increases, thereby raising corporate saving. And, even when dividend increases result (or net proprietors' income rises), part of the resulting increase in disposable personal income is saved. Michael Boskin estimates the elasticity of saving in the U.S. to be 0.4; that is, when business net returns rise by 1 percent, saving rises by 0.4 percent.[11] In the full employment zone, however, the volume of real saving constrains the amount of investment that can be undertaken, so further increases in real investment would require measures to promote saving.

A number of studies of capital requirements in the years ahead have concluded that if we are to increase capital per worker and productivity in line with past trends *and* meet various social goals, including greater energy independence, the ratio of business-fixed investment to GNP must be increased significantly from the average of 10.5 percent for the 1965–75 decade. (The ratio for 1978 was also 10.5 percent.) The study of the Bureau of Economic Analysis concluded that a 12 percent ratio is needed, and this is also the figure targeted in the *Joint Economic Report*, 1979 (Recommendation No. 25).[12] Policy recommendations to increase saving as well as investment are described below.

The diversity of policy options available to influence business investment is indicated by the complex nature of the investment decision. Economists believe that capital outlays are made only if the expected net after-tax return on the investments exceeds the cost (rental price) of capital. The after-tax rate of return depends on the before-tax return and the effective rate of business income taxes. The rental price of capital depends on the relative prices of capital goods, interest rates, the cost of equity financing, and the definition of allowable costs for tax purposes, particularly depreciation charges. Because the volume of saving affects interest rates, it influences investment in this way as well as limiting the available resources for capital formation. Also, because expectations are involved, business confidence is also a factor.

This section is confined to business investment; government out-

11. See Michael J. Boskin, "Taxation, Saving, and the Rate of Interest," *Journal of Political Economy*, April 1978, pp. 3–27.
12. "We agree with the Council of Economic Advisers that further steps to strengthen investment are needed. We favor policies that will raise real business fixed investment to 12 percent of real GNP," *Joint Economic Report*, 1979, p. 61.

lays for capital goods are treated under Increasing the Net Contribution of Government, p. 92. But governmental deficits or surpluses affect total saving and interest rates, so fiscal policy is mentioned here as well as private saving.

Improving the investment climate. A variety of measures can be taken for improving the climate for investment.

RECOMMENDATION ONE

The federal government should adopt a combination of policy measures in the following areas that would improve the business investment climate:

a. *Promotion of productivity growth by the types of policies recommended in this paper, which would accelerate economic growth generally and help in the deceleration of inflation;*

b. *Application of counter-cyclical measures that would increase the stability of economic growth; and*

c. *Containment of government intervention in the economy (regulations, etc.) to situations in which benefits clearly exceed costs, public and private.*

Long-term investments require business confidence that the government understands the need for adequate profit rates in our type of economy, and that it is effectively addressing serious economic problems such as excessive regulation, energy shortages, trade deficits, economic recession, and inflation. As the 1979 Annual Report of the Council of Economic Advisers stated:

> Perhaps the most important single contribution to this objective (increasing investment) would be lower inflation. Expectations that the inflation rate would decline steadily over the next five years would directly attack one of the obstacles to the recovery of business investment, since the uncertainty faced by business has been a major deterrent to investment planning. Indirectly, reduced inflation would have even larger effects on financial markets. With declining inflation, we could look forward confidently to a marked fall in short- and long-term interest rates, to strongly rising stock prices, and hence to a reduction in the cost of both debt and equity capital.[13]

Along with restrained monetary expansion and fiscal policy, the acceleration of productivity advance must be a major part of anti-inflationary policy. Thus, Recommendation One really involves the

13. Council of Economic Advisers, op. cit., p. 117.

entire set of following recommendations, particularly those in Volume Factors (p. 89) and Increasing the Net Contribution of Government (p. 92). Further, once effective policies are in place, governments must pursue a steady-as-you-go course without frequent or erratic changes in policies and their applications that introduce uncertainty into business plans and thus inhibit investment. Reasonably predictable public policies contribute to business confidence in the future, increasing investment demand and economic growth.

Increasing returns on investments. Rates of return should be increased.

RECOMMENDATION TWO

Rates of return on new investment should be increased to an adequate level—defined as one that will induce sufficient investment to offset the voluntary savings of the community at a reasonably full-employment level of national income and product—by a combination of policy measures, recommendations 3–5 below.

During the eight-year period 1970–1977, adjusted domestic after-tax profits of U.S. nonfinancial corporations averaged 4.25 percent of the sector's gross product, compared with a 7.75 percent average for 1947–69.[14] The 1978 ratio was close to the 1970–77 average, but the 1979 ratio will drop significantly. In this computation by George Terborgh based on U.S. Department of Commerce data, the profits estimates were adjusted to revalue inventory and capital consumption charges to current replacement costs. When net worth is adjusted likewise to reflect the revaluation of plant and equipment, the 1970–77 average rate of return is 3.35 percent compared with 5.90 for 1947–69. Most of the decline was due to a drop of before-tax profit rates, rather than increases in the average effective corporate tax rate.

The decline in profit margins resulted in part from the fact that most corporate managements did not adjust pricing policies, to the extent that they had some discretion in pricing, to fully reflect the effects of accelerating inflation on unit costs. More important has been the use of macroeconomic policies to restrain inflation by ultimately holding price increases below unit-cost increases in high-level years—

14. George Terborgh, *Corporate Earning Power in the Seventies: A Disaster* (Washington: Machinery and Allied Products Institute, August 1977). See also Herman I. Liebling, *U.S. Corporate Profitability and Capital Formation: Are Rates of Return Sufficient?* (Elmsford, N.Y.: Pergamon Press, Fall 1979). Liebling's answer is "no," as a result of long-term structural changes.

notably 1966, 1969, 1973–74, and again in 1979. The wage-price controls of 1971–74 and the present voluntary standards also served to limit profit margins. In any case, if investment growth is to be more vigorous in the 1980s than in the 1970s, profit margins must be raised.

RECOMMENDATION THREE
Macroeconomic supply and demand policies should attempt to permit average prices to rise in relation to average unit costs to attain a gross-profit margin consistent with an adequate after-tax rate of return, given the present or prospective set of effective tax rates on business income.

The disadvantage of permitting prices to rise faster than the recent trend rate of increases in unit costs is a temporarily higher rate of price inflation than would prevail with stable profit margins. Once margins were adjusted, however, prices would rise no faster than unit costs. But a more attractive approach is to decelerate the increase in unit costs relative to the recent trend rate of prices. Once profit margins were adequate, price inflation could decelerate in line with unit costs. The deceleration of unit costs could come by incomes policies that would reduce wage-rate increases closer to the increases in output per hour, or by acceleration of productivity increases. With respect to the latter approach, all the policy prescriptions in this paper are relevant.

Because accelerating productivity growth will take time and will be promoted by higher profits and business investment over the short and medium term, serious consideration must be accorded the options for reducing effective business income tax rates.

RECOMMENDATION FOUR
The average effective tax rate on corporate profits should be reduced by one or more of the following measures:
a. Increase depreciation allowances
1) Shorten lives of depreciable assets for tax purposes, as in the 10-5-3 formula of the Jones-Conable bill (see below).
2) Index depreciation charges from acquisition to replacement costs of the structures and equipment.
b. Increase the investment tax credit, possibly from 10 to 12 percent, and expand its coverage to include new nonresidential construction.
c. Reduce the corporate income tax rate.

d. Reduce or eliminate the double taxation of dividends by partial or complete deductibility of dividends from the corporate profits tax base. Further study should be given the several methods of integrating the personal and corporate income taxes as an alternative way of eliminating double taxation of dividends.

RECOMMENDATION FIVE

Reduce personal income tax rates for all brackets. In particular, the 50 percent top marginal rate on income from labor services, set by the Tax Reform Act of 1969, should be extended to "unearned" income from property, which is still subject to a 70 percent maximum rate.

DRI, Inc., prepared an analysis of the relative efficacy and costs of the three options for reducing the effective tax rate on corporate profits.[15] (In this context, the deductibility of dividends may be viewed as a means of reducing the corporate tax rate.) Assuming a $2 billion "tax expenditure" (revenue loss) in the first year from revising each, the fifth year the cost of further acceleration of depreciation allowances would rise to about $7.2 billion; the cost of an increased investment tax credit would rise to about $5.3 billion; and the cost of the corporate tax rate reduction would be about $3 billion. The estimated average stimulus over the five-year period per dollar of revenue loss from each would be 1.14, 0.69, and 0.11, respectively. Other investigations, including an econometric model simulation by the Congressional Budget Office, show accelerated depreciation and the expanded investment tax credit having about the same effect.[16] Virtually all studies agree that each of these two measures would have a significantly larger "bang for a buck" than a reduction in the corporate profits tax rate. That is partly because the latter measure would decrease the effect of the investment tax credit and of depreciation (and interest) deductibility. Further, the latter two measures produce benefits dependent on the amount of new investment, whereas the effects of reduced corporate tax rates depend on net income from old as well as new assets.

15. See testimony of Allen Sinai of DRI, Inc. "Tax Expenditures, Business Capital Spending, and Productivity" in Hearings on Tax Expenditures, Committee on Ways and Means, Subcommittee on Oversight, March 27, 1979.

16. Congressional Budget Office, *The Economic Outlook,* A Report to the Senate and House Committees on the Budget, Part II (Washington: Government Printing Office, February 1978), pp. 47–49.

Accelerating depreciation stimulates longer-lived investments, whereas the investment tax credit stimulates short-term investments. This fact would seem to make accelerated depreciation the most attractive alternative at this time, because fixed investment was heavily concentrated in short-run projects for much of expansion period following the 1973–75 downturn.

At this time (fall 1979) proponents of accelerated depreciation appear to be joining forces to support the Jones-Conable bill, which has more than one hundred cosponsors. Under this measure, firms could write off the cost of new structures in ten years, equipment in five, and automobiles and light trucks in three. The 10-5-3 formula is estimated to reduce business income tax liabilities by $5 billion the first full year, subsequently rising to $30 billion.[17] But much of the first-round loss to the Treasury would be made up by the increased revenue from "reflows" rising from the multiplier effect on income of the increased investment, not to mention the greater growth of supply capacity to the extent that productivity growth is stimulated.

A *dividend-paid* credit for corporations would have basically the same effect as an equivalent *dividend-received* credit discussed in the next subsection. In addition to reducing the effective rate of corporate income tax, it would raise the return to equity, because dividends would qualify as an expensible cost, just as interest on debt is at present, so corporations would tend to shift more toward equity financing. This shift is desirable in view of the large increases in debt ratios in recent years. Note, however, that the dividend-paid credit applies to all dividends regardless of the categories of shareholders, whereas the dividend-received credit could be limited to domestic individual residents and exclude foreign shareholders, unions, charities, and other fiduciaries.

A partial credit is more likely of enactment than a full credit. Even a 30 percent dividend credit would have reduced the tax on corporate source income by about $6.8 billion in 1978, the equivalent of a 5 percentage point reduction in the average effective tax rate on corporate source income.[18] On a personal basis, the reduction tends to be progressive in incidence. A full credit would create strong pressures on corporations to pay out all their net income, resulting, in effect, in full integration of the personal and corporate taxes. The impact of

17. Art Pine, "Depreciation Speedup Embraced," *The Washington Post*, August 12, 1979.
18. See Martin S. Feldstein, *Corporate Tax Integration: A Quantitative Comparison of Alternatives* (New York: Tax Foundation, Inc., December 1977), p. 5.

integration depends on what other changes are made in tax laws, of course, and the effect of any dividend credit plan depends to a considerable degree on how firms respond in adjusting their dividends. That is why we called for further study before enactment of integration legislation.

The proposed reduction of personal income tax rates would increase the after-tax return on capital investments by the self-employed, proprietors and business partners, as well as on financial investments by individuals, and would tend to increase saving generally, because not all of the increase in disposable personal income would be spent on consumption. The cut should apply to all income groups, because previous cuts have tended to increase progressivity of income taxes. The fact that most saving is done by persons in higher income brackets suggests that a reduction in progressivity would stimulate saving—but this argument must be weighed against equity considerations.

The 70 percent maximum rate on property income versus a 50 percent tax rate on labor income clearly discriminates against saving and investment, and the 50 percent maximum rate should be legislated to apply to both as soon as possible.

Reducing the explicit or implicit cost of financing new investment. Several measures are recommended for reducing these costs.

RECOMMENDATION SIX

Congress should pursue policies that would tend to raise equity prices and reduce the cost of equity financing.

As pointed out in the 1979 Annual Report of the Council of Economic Advisers, the ratio of market value (equity plus interest-bearing debt) to current replacement cost of the net assets of non-financial corporations declined from 1.23 for 1962–66 to .70 in 1978.[19] This decline had an adverse effect on new investment. So, too, did the 1969 and 1976 increases in the capital gains tax, which dried up funds for financing new and speculative, growth-oriented companies.

RECOMMENDATION SEVEN

In addition to recommendations 1–5, Congress should enact legislation providing more favorable treatment of capital gains:
a. "Rollover" treatment that would not tax capital gains when proceeds from sales of assets are reinvested.
b. Reduction or elimination of capital gains taxation.

19. *1979 Annual Report* of the Council of Economic Advisers, p. 128.

c. *Taxation of only that part of capital gains that represents appreciation greater than the increase in the CPI over the holding period.*

d. *Liberalization of loss carry-forward and carry-back provisions.*

RECOMMENDATION EIGHT
Congress should reduce the double taxation of dividends by increasing the $100 dividend exclusion, or by providing partial credits against dividends received.

RECOMMENDATION NINE
Reduce the real interest rate by encouraging saving.

The measures under Rates of Return on New Investments, above, designed to increase after-tax corporate profits would also increase corporate saving (retained earnings), because increases in dividend payments generally lag increases in net income; and reduced personal income tax rates would increase personal saving. In addition, the following measures could be considered.

RECOMMENDATION TEN
Eliminate Regulation Q and permit interest rates on savings accounts to be determined competitively.

RECOMMENDATION ELEVEN
Reduce the rate of taxation of interest by exempting some proportion or amount of interest received; or by taxing only that part which represents a higher rate on the value of the principal at the beginning of the tax-year than the rate of increase in the CPI during the year.

RECOMMENDATION TWELVE
Tax incentives for personal saving should be strengthened. Tax deferral for saving up to some maximum, as under Keogh and IRA plans, could be extended to other groups. Tax exemption or deferral for income from capital (as in provisions relating to pension, profit-sharing, and stock bonus plans) could be broadened to include other types of plans, such as for dividend reinvestment.

RECOMMENDATION THIRTEEN
Federal, state, and local governments should attempt to run budget surpluses on current account when the economy is operating at high employment rates and private investment demand is strong.

The cost of equity financing can be reduced by measures that would increase stock prices, as by reducing the effective tax-rate on corporate-source income and further reducing the capital gains tax (because appreciation is part of the total return on equity investment). The need is evident in view of the significant increases in business debt-equity ratios and the decline in interest coverage of earnings. These developments since the early 1960s make business much more vulnerable to recessions and temporary setbacks, because debt carries fixed charges while equity does not. Ways of increasing after-tax business income had been discussed in Rules of Return on New Investments, above, but Recommendation Eight is listed as an alternative to the dividend-paid credit. A dividend-received credit has the advantage of making equity investments more immediately attractive to investors, thus augmenting the buying incentive that would stem from the reduction in the effective corporate tax rate. The present $100 dividend exclusion now costs the Treasury about $450 million a year.

The 1969 and 1976 increases in the capital gains tax rates strengthened the "lock-in" effect of such taxes, reducing the effectiveness of the liquidity function of equity markets. As Feldstein has shown, capital gains realizations are highly sensitive to the tax; sales by equity holders in higher income brackets dropped significantly after 1969. Likewise, investments in new venture capital firms slowed to a trickle. Because the 1978 tax reform partially restored the pre-1969 rates, the financing of new growth-oriented companies has increased significantly.[20] Additional reductions in capital gains tax rates would have a further beneficial effect; proponents of this approach argue that revenues from the tax would not decline as realizations increase.

With respect to measures that encourage saving and thus tend to reduce the interest rate, some economists have advocated exempting net saving from the personal income tax altogether as a means of redressing the antisaving bias of income taxation (see Value-added Tax, below). That is not recommended, in part because of the difficulties for individuals of estimating that part of the change in their net worth due to net saving during the tax year, and for the Internal Revenue Service in auditing the estimates. Instead, a number of proposals for exempting part or all of specific kinds of saving or

20. See *Building a Better Future—Economic Choices for the 1980s* (New York: New York Stock Exchange, Fall 1979).

property income are listed. (Note that Keogh and IRA plans cost the Treasury less than $2 billion in FY 1979.)

With respect to Recommendation Thirteen, economists agree that deficit financing by governments tends to "crowd out" some private investment by raising interest rates. Conversely, government surpluses help ease pressures on interest rates and facilitate business investment. The federal government, in particular, should continue to exercise restraint in planning expenditure increases, so that a surplus will emerge when the economy returns to the full employment zone.

Value-added tax. The use of a value-added tax should be explored.

RECOMMENDATION FOURTEEN

Serious consideration and study should be given to the enactment of a value-added tax (exempting capital goods) if required to make up the net loss of revenue from the proposed reductions of effective income tax rates and other adjustments, in order to provide a full-employment surplus in the federal government.

The advantage of a value-added tax is that it is relatively neutral with respect to decisions to spend on consumption goods or to save and invest, if capital goods are exempt from the tax. In this respect it is superior to income taxes that discriminate against saving and investment. As Ture and Sanden point out, both the returns from saving and income out of which saving is made are taxed, which represents a form of double taxation.[21] To state it differently, income taxes reduce disposable income and thus reduce both consumption and saving; but because the returns from the investments into which savings flow are also taxed, the present value of investment is reduced, making saving and investment less attractive relative to consumption than would be the case under a neutral tax system. As Martin Feldstein views it, income taxes put a wedge between the average before-tax rate of return on investment and the net rate received by savers, thus reducing saving below the optimum proportion of income.[22] He also argues that the present U.S. social security system reduces saving.

21. See Norma T. Ture and B. Kenneth Sanden, *The Effects of Tax Policy on Capital Formation* (New York: Financial Executives Research Foundation, 1977).

22. This argument is developed by Martin S. Feldstein, "National Saving in the United States," Capital for Production Jobs. (Englewood Cliffs, N.J.: Prentice-Hall for the American Assembly, 1977).

Capital recovery allowances ameliorate but do not eliminate the disproportionate burden of income taxes on saving, particularly with inflation, as do certain tax loopholes. But some non-income taxes accentuate the antisaving bias. This is true of capital gains taxes. Because future increases in returns from capital will be taxed as they accrue, taxing the capitalized value of the expected increases is another layer of taxation on the same income stream. Estate, inheritance, and gift taxes are similar to capital gains taxes. Property taxes also add to the burden on saving because they are the equivalent of taxes on the explicit or implicit income from the property.

Ture and Sanden maintain that the antisaving bias of the U.S. tax system could be eliminated by integrating the personal and corporate income taxes and by excluding current saving from the individual income tax base. The revenue loss could be made up by increasing tax rates on personal income less saving, or by substituting the value-added tax, which is essentially neutral with respect to saving-consumption decisions.

The recommendations in the previous sections move in the directions indicated but do not go all the way, partly because of the administrative problems noted earlier. Also, although the value-added tax is neutral on saving decisions, it is regressive—although that feature could be reduced by exempting certain necessities. But if only partial reliance were placed on the value-added tax, whatever progressivity were desired by Congress could be accomplished through the traditional income tax. And the antisaving bias of the income tax could be largely neutralized by the various measures proposed in recommendations 2–13.

Accelerating productivity growth and reducing prices. Policy measures could be devised to accelerate productivity growth in the capital goods industries, thus reducing their relative prices and stimulating capital outlays.

RECOMMENDATION FIFTEEN

A higher investment tax credit should be granted capital goods manufacturers than prevails generally—e.g., 15 percent compared with the present 10 percent on equipment outlays.

RECOMMENDATION SIXTEEN

Capital goods producers should be given priority in other measures designed to promote productivity, where applicable.

This approach may seem novel, but because the prices of capital goods are one of the determinants of investment, special measures to stimulate productivity growth in these industries would mean lower prices than would otherwise prevail, and thus would stimulate capital outlays. A higher investment tax credit for capital goods manufacturers has been proposed elsewhere,[23] and would cost close to $1 billion. The exemption of capital goods from the proposed value-added tax is an example of another kind of measure to favor this key sector of the economy. For another example, priority could be given to the formation of industry productivity committees in capital goods industries and to the promotion of productivity improvement programs in the firms of these industries and their major suppliers (see Improving Labor Efficiency and Other Factors, p. 99).

Promoting advances in technological knowledge and innovation

Research and development activities are undoubtedly the fountainhead of technological progress in this modern era. Proposals for stimulating R&D expenditures and activities are highlighted in the first subsection. Subsequent subsections consider the patent system, which affects the profitability of R&D and innovation; the gathering and dissemination of scientific and technological information, which help promote and diffuse innovations; government procurement policy, which can be used as a lever to spur innovation; and the role of small technology-based firms, which contribute disproportionately to technological advance.

Policies to increase R&D activities. The new processes and producers' goods that result from formal and informal R&D activities are a major element in raising total factor productivity, as shown in Table 2. Even the introduction of new and improved consumer goods, though inadequately reflected in output and productivity measures, contribute to productivity growth through the learning-curve effect, because productivity generally rises faster in the early stages of producing new goods than in later stages when expansion of the market slows. Because the decline in R&D outlays relative to GNP after the mid-1960s and the consequent slowing in advances in technological knowledge and knowhow were major elements in the productivity slowdown, various measures that could be employed to increase real R&D expenditures should be examined.

23. See John W. Kendrick, "Productivity and Business," in Jules Backman, ed.

Almost half of R&D is federally financed, though the effect on civilian technology is less, despite spillovers, because the major portion of federal funding is for direct national security purposes. Nevertheless, the decline in federal R&D after 1968 had an adverse effect on technological progress. Also, government policy on private R&D influences that portion of the total. Under present law, business R&D outlays may be charged to current expense, despite their investment characteristics. A good case can be made for still more favorable treatment based on the externalities of inventions resulting from R&D, the major uncertainties of most projects, and the indivisibilities of many. A number of research studies indicate that while private rates of return to R&D are higher than those on tangible investments, social rates of return on R&D are more than twice the private rates.[24]

Further, R&D outlays help to raise rates of return on tangible investments, while increases in tangible investment tend to increase the demand for R&D activity. Despite its key role, however, R&D generally represents a much smaller portion of the total cost of producing innovations than the subsequent tangible investments.

Of the policy options, tax incentives for R&D generally have the advantage of leaving decisions as to the allocation of R&D among projects up to private managements that are skilled in assessing relative profit prospects. Selective support by government for applied research and development may be indicated for projects in which there are important externalities, costs or risks are high, industry structure is fragmented, or the industries are strategic in national economic policy considerations.

RECOMMENDATION SEVENTEEN
Federal government funding of basic and applied R&D in constant dollars should be gradually and predictably increased.

As a rough rule of thumb, real R&D outlays should increase at least in proportion to the trend-rate of growth in real GNP, currently estimated by the Council of Economic Advisers to be about 3.5 percent a year. This figure may be considered a minimum in view of the higher rates of return on R&D than on tangible investment. Basic as well as applied R&D must be expanded. Although basic research has little effect on productivity in the short run, scientific advances

24. See *Relationships Between R&D and Economic Growth/Productivity* (Washington: National Science Foundation, November 9, 1977).

are drawn on by R&D. Most basic research is financed by the federal government, and most of that is performed in universities and independent laboratories. Predictability is important because of the long lead time required for the education of scientists and engineers.

RECOMMENDATION EIGHTEEN

The present investment tax credit for equipment should be expanded to cover business expenditures for R&D. The definition of R&D as set forth by the National Science Foundation or the Financial Accounting Standards Board could be used, or an alternative definition spelled out in the legislation. This would cost about $2 billion in FY 1980.

RECOMMENDATION NINETEEN

As an alternative to Recommendation Eighteen, a tax credit of more than 10 percent (say 25 percent) could be granted on increases in R&D over the level of the previous year. This approach would be less costly (about $0.5 billion) and possibly more effective in eliciting expansion of R&D activities.

RECOMMENDATION TWENTY

The present investment tax credit for laboratory equipment purchases should be expanded to include new construction, and consideration should be given to the full expensing of such outlays for tax purposes.

RECOMMENDATION TWENTY-ONE

As an alternative to tax credits generally—and certainly for firms with no net income—grants (direct subsidies) for R&D performance and capital outlays could be made in the same proportions as tax credits.

RECOMMENDATION TWENTY-TWO

A federal government organization to support cooperative business-university R&D projects should be established.

The blueprint contained in S. 1250, "a bill to promote U.S. technological innovation for the achievement of national economic, environmental, and social goals, and for other purposes," could serve as a basis for such an approach. It establishes an Office of Industrial Technology in the Department of Commerce. The office would identify technological needs and opportunities, make recommendations to the President and Congress on measures to promote innovation, and provide assistance for the establishment of Centers for Industrial Technology involving participation of persons from industry and universities in cooperative technology innovation projects. In addition to supporting innovation activities, the Office and Centers would promote education and training of individuals in innovational processes, and improve mechanisms for dissemination of scientific and technological information. In some cases, grants might be made to industry associations or consortia of small firms on a matching basis, for cooperative R&D (possibly requiring exemption from antitrust laws). Presidential recommendations in this area, based on the recently completed report of his committee for domestic policy review of technological innovation, may be forthcoming. (See Addendum B.)

Revising the patent system to promote invention and innovations. The patent system has been an important method for providing incentives for R&D, invention, and commercial product and process innovations. Preceding the leveling out of the ratio of business R&D to GNP, the total number of patents issued annually declined after 1971; although, based on filing dates, the downward trend has been slight. The share of patents issued to foreign applicants has doubled in the past fourteen years, indicating increasing technological competition from abroad. Most patents in high technology areas are granted to corporations; individuals own relatively more in areas requiring less innovational expense. Small firms produce innovations at a higher rate than large firms and put a higher percentage of their patented inventions to commercial use. Small-firm patents have a greater effect in increasing sales than those of larger firms, which seem to enjoy an advantage in cost-reducing innovations.

Rates of return on patented inventions vary over a wide range. There is a strong correlation between exporting and R&D in the United States. There is a positive trade balance in technology-intensive goods and a negative balance in other goods. There is also a positive trade balance in technology transfer (license fees and royalties, etc.). Patent filings abroad appear to enhance exports.

The U.S. patent system is basically sound and has well performed its constitutional mandate "to promote the progress of . . . useful arts." Nevertheless, several studies have concluded that the patent system could be srengthened to do a better job in promoting decisions to commercialize inventions. Recently, the Advisory Subcommittee on

Patent and Information Policy of the Advisory Committee on Industrial Innovation, convened by the Secretary of Commerce, made various recommendations, upon which the Forum has drawn. In general terms, the subcommittee, composed of patent attorneys and other experts on the subject, concluded that investments to commercialize inventions can be encouraged by reducing the risks and costs involved. Risks could be reduced if the inventions were covered by reliable patents and if uncertainties in the utilization of patent rights could be resolved quickly and inexpensively. The subcommittee also noted that availability of reliable patents encourages decisions to disclose inventions in patents, which appears to stimulate competitive R&D. Other conclusions are reflected in the recommendations listed below. The subcommittee also recommended study of the possibilities of extending patent rights to presently unpatentable technological advances, such as new life forms, for industrial applications and computer software.[25]

RECOMMENDATION TWENTY-THREE
Congress should:
a. Lengthen the period of patent protection from seventeen to twenty years. (The British recently lengthened the term of patent protection from eighteen to twenty years.) or
b. Extend the patent term to compensate for delays in commercialization of patented inventions due to federal regulations.

RECOMMENDATION TWENTY-FOUR
Commercial rights to inventions made under government contract or research support should be structured in a manner capable of being transferred to the firms or individuals responsible in order to promote investments in their development. License rights would be reserved by the government to ensure no further payment for government use of such inventions.

RECOMMENDATION TWENTY-FIVE
Improve reliability of the patent grant by:
a. Strengthening the Patent and Trademark Office (PTO) to assure rigorous, high-quality examinations and providing modern search tools that increase the probability of finding the relevant

25. Industry representatives also favor implementation of the recommendations of CONTU (National Commission on New Technological Uses of Copyright Works) with respect to software, data bases, and photocopying.

prior art, reduce search costs, and reduce the frequency of subsequent legal proceedings.

b. *Provide a reexamination process, available to all interested parties, to ensure that the patentability of the invention described in the patent had been considered by the Patent Office in the light of all relevant prior publications.*

c. *Provide a central court to hear patent appeals to ensure greater consistency in judicial decisions, thereby reducing uncertainty.*

RECOMMENDATION TWENTY-SIX

To reduce enforcement costs, the Supreme Court and the Judicial Conference should be requested to require each federal court to exercise a high degree of control over the conduct of patent litigations, with express concern for the time and expense of discovery.

RECOMMENDATION TWENTY-SEVEN

The statutory standard of patentability should be clarified and licensees permitted to agree not to attack the validity of licensed patents.

RECOMMENDATION TWENTY-EIGHT

The State Department should adopt the policy of encouraging other countries to provide U.S. innovators the right to obtain enforceable patent rights, thus augmenting the incentive to commercialize U.S. innovations in international markets.

Expanding the dissemination of scientific and technological information. The publication and dissemination of scientific and technological information, an important aspect of the diffusion of innovations, significantly affect the rate of productivity advance. The private sector disseminates a tremendous amount of relevant information through books, articles in professional and trade journals, advertising materials, data banks, and so forth. But the federal government also plays a major role as a creator and distributor of information. In addition to the patent applications, technical information, and research reports written or collected by the various departments and agencies, there are reports on research funded by NSF and other agencies; census reports; bibliographical data; reports of commercial and scientific attachés; and so on. The Government Printing Office, the National Technical Information Service (NTIS), and the agencies themselves make most of the information available. But despite the relatively open policy of the federal government (except for limitations imposed by considerations of national security and of individual and corporate privacy), there are still problems of accessibility, timeliness, and cost.

Of particular importance is the need to expand the collection and dissemination of scientific and technological information from abroad. More than two-thirds of all R&D is now done outside the United States, and the productivity of an increasing number of industries in certain other countries is catching up with and even surpassing levels in the United States. Now is the time to make the international flow of information and technology more of a two-way proposition—into as well as out of the United States. In some cases, intergovernment cooperative arrangements could be helpful.

RECOMMENDATION TWENTY-NINE

The Patent and Trademark Office should complete the development of an effective computer-based search and retrieval system and support the development of appropriate classification and indexing schemes. It should also require submission of supplemental information about a patent's characteristics, use, and potential applications to make accessing easier and more complete. The PTO should also strengthen its depository library system and install its automated search system in key locations. It should consider providing instruction and assistance, particularly to individuals and small firms, in use of the system.

RECOMMENDATION THIRTY

The Worldwide Information and Trade System (WITS) at the Department of Commerce should be strengthened by industry representation and by staffing overseas commercial facilities with better qualified commercial officers. Expanded trade and marketing information helps in development of appropriate technologies. Further, WITS should make arrangements to collect and disseminate information about foreign regulations, standards, and requirements necessary to obtain product approval and certification for the distribution and use of such products in the various countries.

RECOMMENDATION THIRTY-ONE

The federal government should augment its efforts to encourage international technology transfer by pursuing negotiations within international bodies such as UNCTAD and OECD; by resisting restrictive regulations on technology transfer by individual foreign countries or international agencies; and by clearly stating its intent to continue to permit cross-licensing agreements between U.S. companies and their Western subsidiaries and affiliates.

RECOMMENDATION THIRTY-TWO

The program of the Office of Technology Assessment and Forecast of the PTO that provides information related to areas of high technology in foreign countries should be expanded; the PTO should obtain complete foreign patent information, and dissemination should be made by NTIS. Further, NTIS should also disseminate abstracts or reports of R&D activities sponsored by foreign governments as it now does for U.S. sponsored technical reports, assuming the exchange of such reports can be negotiated.

RECOMMENDATION THIRTY-THREE

It should be federal government policy that agencies receiving or collecting nonconfidential technical information should make it conveniently available at incremental cost, either directly to users or through private firms prepared to add value by such means as indexing, abstracting, reformating, arranging, combining, packaging, and distributing.

Using procurement policies to promote innovation. Procurement offers a powerful lever, through use of incentives and penalties, for promoting innovation on the part of major suppliers. As the largest single sector of the economy, with procurement in excess of $50 billion a year, the federal government is in a particularly strategic position to use this lever, and indeed has done so. But the combined purchases from private industry of state and local governments are almost double those of Washington, so there are opportunities for the Office of Federal Procurement Policy to share its expertise with those governmental units. It is also conceivable that private firms could improve their purchasing policies to stimulate their suppliers to do a better job of reducing real costs per unit of output and improving quality. And the consumer movement, with its emphasis on quality, may have neglected the cost side of the equation.

An early example of federal government procurement policy was the contracts with airlines to carry airmail. A recent example is NASA's contract with Comsat to provide worldwide communications for NASA's tracking network. Currently, contracts for solar installations on government buildings are promoting the development of new technology. In the mid-1970s, the Experimental Technology Incentives Program in the Bureau of Standards conducted successful projects in collaboration with a number of agencies to reduce costs or improve products (e.g., lawnmowers, water heaters, and air-conditioners) by use of policies involving performance rather than product specifications, two-step procurement (evaluation of technical proposals by manufacturers prior to cost proposals), purchase of prototypes, life cycle costing as a basis for procurement awards, and sharing of cost saving with producers in some contracts.

A related approach was embodied in OMB Circular No. A-109, "Major Systems Acquisitions" (April 5, 1976), which improved procurement methods by, for example (1) expressing needs and program objectives in mission terms and not in equipment terms to encourage innovation and creative competition, and (2) emphasizing the initial activities of the system acquisition process to allow competitive exploration of alternative system design concepts in response to mission needs. The Advisory Subcommittee on Federal Procurement Policy of the Domestic Policy Review Committee felt that a general policy of stimulating innovation in federal procurement of common-use items as well as of system components would be constructive.

RECOMMENDATION THIRTY-FOUR

The Office of Federal Procurement Policy (OFPP) should develop, issue, and execute a policy statement that establishes the goal of stimulating innovation through procurement techniques. In consultation with the Department of Commerce and the General Services Administration, the OFPP would promote techniques such as providing a market for innovative products in their early stages, applying the principles of OMB Circular A-109 to procurement of common-use items, setting performance standards, and other methods proved effective by the Experimental Technological Incentives Program.

RECOMMENDATION THIRTY-FIVE

Contracting personnel in GSA should be made more aware of product and other technological developments in their fields by instruction and a broadened exchange of information between industry and government. One official should be assigned the procurement function in each agency and should propose new purchases that would significantly encourage innovation in areas important to the agency's mission for review by OFPP and OMB.

RECOMMENDATION THIRTY-SIX

The Office of Federal Procurement Policy should be prepared to consult with state and local governments and their associations to share its developing expertise on methods for stimulating innovations by suppliers to reduce costs or improve quality.

Promoting small, technology-based enterprises. Small firms based on new or advanced technology have contributed more to technological progress than their size would indicate and have also helped strengthen the forces of competition. They have often been founded by scientists, engineers, and other officials of large companies who see opportunities for more rapid exploitation of new technologies than is likely in the larger firms. A major economic incentive is the prospect of rapid growth and the appreciation of founders shares or options.

The dollar volume of new equity issues of new companies dwindled to virtually nothing in the 1970s, due in part to the 1969 and 1976 increase in the capital gains tax and the general doldrums of the stock markets, reflecting erosion of profit margins after adjustment for the effects of inflation. Recommendations 1–16 would help small as well as large firms. But in view of the invigorating role of small technological enterprises, a case can be made for special measures to promote their founding and growth up to the point where they are fully competitive, given the existence of that potential initially.

RECOMMENDATION THIRTY-SEVEN

For small technology-based businesses, properly defined, allow more favorable stock option incentives to founders and key personnel by (a) increasing the qualified options time from five to ten years, and (b) postponing the tax on income derived from the exercise of nonqualified options until the shares have been sold rather than at the time of exercise.

RECOMMENDATION THIRTY-EIGHT

Allow tax-free rollover of equity investments in small technology-based enterprises and permit start-up operating losses to flow through to founding investors.

RECOMMENDATION THIRTY-NINE

The Securities and Exchange Commission should further simplify regulations under Rule 146 (private placement of small investments) and increase its Regulation A limits on the size of investment offerings that are not subject to the full regulations at least to reflect the effects of inflation.

RECOMMENDATION FORTY

Encourage "lone-wolf" types of inventors and small technology-based enterprises by selective procurement policies and by assistance in complying with environmental, safety, and other mandated social regulations.

RECOMMENDATION FORTY-ONE

The Small Business Administration should substantially expand its direct loans and financial assistance to small business investment companies (SBICs) that provide debt and equity capital to newer small businesses. The latter is particularly important in view of the higher debt-equity ratios for small corporations (those with under $5 million of assets) than for larger ones.[26]

Increasing the quality of labor

Intangible investments in humans are the chief means of increasing the quality and productivity of the employed labor force. Of these, by far the most important is investment in education and training to increase the knowledge and know-how, which not only raises productivity but also the satisfaction from work and from life generally. Quantitatively less important for raising productivity but even more basic for the enjoyment of living are investments in medical and health care. Sometimes the costs associated with labor mobility are treated as human investment, but this variable is covered in Facilitating Reallocations of Labor and Capital, p. 86. Another topic is the changing composition of the employed labor force, which affects productivity because various categories of labor have differing productivities reflected in differential rates of remuneration.

Policies to increase the quantity and quality of education and training per worker. The traditional faith of Americans in education as a means of promoting the economic progress of individuals and the nation, as well as producing better citizens, is well founded. A number of studies have established that private rates of return on educational outlays are comparable with those on tangible capital outlays.[27] Not only does additional education and training permit individuals to obtain (or create) higher paying jobs, on average, but it enables

26. A more extensive set of measures to aid small business is contained in a report of the SBA Office of Advocacy Task Force, *Small Business and Innovation* (Washington: U.S. Small Business Administration, May 1979).

27. See Gary Becker, *Human Capital* (New York: National Bureau of Economic Research, 1965).

them to perform more efficiently in the same job and under less supervision. Education permits individuals a wider choice of occupations and increases mobility. It makes individuals more receptive to ideas and more alert to better ways and means of working.

Advancing education and training interact with technological progress. The higher education system produces the scientists and engineers who expand knowledge and make inventions and the managers who make the decisions to commit investment funds for innovation. The increases in complexity of technology increase the demands on the educational system generally to provide the background for young people entering the labor force to adjust and adapt to rising job requirements. They also increase the demands on industry to provide formal and on-the-job training programs for workers to learn specific skills. Investments in these forms of human capital per person have increased steadily over the decades and have made a major contribution to productivity growth.

Some evidence of declining return to educational investments in the 1970s is probably associated with the slowdown in technological progress. Reaccelerating productivity growth would probably help to raise the rate of return on education. The social returns on education, however, are higher than the private monetary returns, and education has a current and future consumption component in addition to its investment characteristics. Continued increases in public and private outlays on education and training therefore seem warranted. Perhaps the main areas in which improvements are to be sought are in the productivity and the quality of the educational and training enterprise, bringing it into closer conformity with current and prospective social and economic requirements and increasing its accessibility. The decline in AGCT scores since the early 1960s bears testimony to the urgency of the need to increase the effectiveness of education.

The productivity of the education community is difficult to measure because of the problems in defining and measuring output units adjusted for quality change.[28] But the concept is nonetheless real, and the need to improve the productivity of education institutions is apparent as a means of holding down increases in unit costs

28. For one attempt, see June O'Neill, "Productivity Trends in Higher Education" in J. Froomkin, D. Jamison, and R. Radner, eds., *Education as an Industry* (Cambridge, Mass.: Bollinger Publishers for the National Bureau of Economic Research, 1976).

and thus student charges and other sources of finance. As far as the administrative, business management, housekeeping and other non-teaching functions of schools and institutions of higher education are concerned, there are many industrial technologies that are applicable, and a greater business input in this area could be helpful in speeding diffusion.

In recent years, there have also been important advances made in teaching technologies, such as computer-assisted instruction and various types of teaching machines, closed-circuit TV, programmed materials, films, tapes, and other teaching aids. But diffusion has been slow, in part because of the fragmented nature of the market, particularly at the local school system level, the conservatism of the teaching profession in this regard, and the lack of pecuniary, market incentives in the public sector. Also, research has lagged on the relative effectiveness of alternative teaching methods using various technologies. There are probable limits to the introduction of new educational technologies, however, particularly in advanced courses. As William G. Bowen has testified:

> Looking ahead, the best hope would seem to be that teaching aids eventually will reduce the real resource costs of providing large-scale instruction in basic subjects, and that the savings achieved in these areas can somehow be used to strengthen the financial capacity of the entire system of higher education to provide the intensive, the individualized instruction which will continue to be required.[29]

Given the knowledge explosion and the rapid pace of technological change, resources devoted to continuing adult education should be expanded. The increasing average age of the population projected for the decades ahead underlines the desirability of this expansion. Selling adult education will be easier if the notion is instilled in school years that learning is a lifelong activity.

After passage of the 1972 Education Amendments, the proportion of appropriated federal funds (which account for about 25 percent of total financial requirements) swung dramatically from institutional aid by means of grants for various purposes to a variety of student aid programs designed especially to help children of low-income families (Basic Educational Opportunity Grants, State Student In-

29. William G. Bowen, "Economic Pressures on the Major Private Universities," *The Economics and Financing of Higher Education in the United States*, A Compendium of Papers Submitted to the Joint Economic Committee, Congress of the United States, 1969.

centive Grants, College Work Study Program, Supplementary Educational Opportunity Grants, and the National Direct Student Loan Program, in addition to social security and veterans educational benefits). These measures have helped increase access, and thus the greater development of potential capacities. They have also—as intended by the proponents of this approach, which included the Carnegie Commission—increased the competition among higher education institutions, which should enhance quality and efficiency, according to the market model. The student aid approach also benefits institutions financially, including the direct grants that are largely tied to the volume of aid provided the students at the various institutions. Special-purpose grants for research, construction, etc., continue but at a real-dollar level below that of the 1960s.

Unfortunately, funding of the student aid programs is below authorizations, and increases would help the realization of their purposes. Some observers also think that categorical grants should be increased.[30] The intricate issues involved need not be discussed here; however, if the purposes of federal higher education policy are to be served, institutional grants should be made with due regard for efficiency and quality as well as to need.

Expansion of student loan programs and tuition tax credits would help middle-income families cope with the financial squeeze inflicted by inflation and the decline in real spendable income.

RECOMMENDATION FORTY-TWO

The National Institute of Education (NIE), in conjunction with other interested federal agencies, should expand its program of support for development of educational technologies and methods, and for research on the relative costs and effectiveness of alternative pedagogical methods and technologies, holding content and educational objectives constant.[31]

RECOMMENDATION FORTY-THREE

The NIE should take a more active role in promoting the diffusion of new, tested educational technologies, possibly including as-

30. See Clifton Conrad and Joseph Cosand, *The Implications of Federal Education Policy*, ERIC/Higher Education Report No. 1 (Washington: American Association for Higher Education, 1976).

31. See Keith Lumsden, "Technological Innovation in a Hostile Environment: Problems of Increasing Productivity in Higher Education," *Productivity in Higher Education* (Washington: National Institute of Education and Office of Education, September 1973).

sistance in developing centralized purchasing arrangements for education institutions at the several levels.

RECOMMENDATION FORTY-FOUR

Universities should require courses in education, including instruction in the use of recent technologies, of all students planning to teach in institutions of higher education, as well as in primary and secondary schools. College and university faculty members who have not been so trained should be required to take special courses in educational methods and techniques, with due regard for maintaining and enhancing the quality of instruction.[32]

RECOMMENDATION FORTY-FIVE

Congress should increase appropriations and funding of federal student aid programs to authorized levels and relax requirements for aid in order to increase further access to postsecondary education.

RECOMMENDATION FORTY-SIX

Tax credits should be instituted for some portion of tuition payments by individuals. Tuition aid provided by employers should be counted as part of the taxable income of its recipients, unless it were patently unrelated to the job.

RECOMMENDATION FORTY-SEVEN

Public funding or guarantees of student loans should be expanded. Although the default rate on such loans is relatively high, the loans can be justified on grounds of both equity and economic efficiency (given the investment characteristics of education).[33]

RECOMMENDATION FORTY-EIGHT

Within school systems, greater emphasis should be placed on aptitude and interest testing prior to student choice of career. Expansion of career counseling is also indicated—advising high school and college students on relative labor market trends and the outlook for particular occupations and professions. In counseling,

32. See D. M. Medley, *Teacher Competence and Teacher Effectiveness. A Review of Process—Product Research* (Washington: American Association of Colleges for Teacher Education, August 1977); also *Finance, Productivity and Management in Postsecondary Education* (Washington: National Institute of Education, 1978).

33. See *Education and Economic Growth* (Washington: National Commission on Productivity, June 1971).

greater use could be made of advising by representatives of business, nonprofit institutions, and governmental agencies and of work-study programs.

RECOMMENDATION FORTY-NINE
Adult education programs, including televised courses and the "open university," should be expanded.

RECOMMENDATION FIFTY
The National Science Foundation should continue to steadily increase grants for basic and applied research to institutions of higher education in order to enable them to better perform their function of training students for scientific research and innovational activities, as well as for knowledge and know-how acquired.

In view of the leveling of college and university enrollments and faculty numbers, increased funds for research would permit an increasing proportion of faculties to combine teaching with research to the benefit of both, as well as aid institutions financially. Increased funding helps speed the incorporation of advances in knowledge into the received body of knowledge that is transmitted by educational processes.

RECOMMENDATION FIFTY-ONE
Either tax credits or matching grants should be provided by the federal government for individual and company contributions for basic or applied research projects at universities and nonprofit research institutions. A portion of the funds could be used for undergraduate university or institutional research, and the participants would retain publication and patent rights.

RECOMMENDATION FIFTY-TWO
Further expansion and strengthening of formal and on-the-job training and development programs, authorized by the Comprehensive Employment and Training Act, are needed. This expansion is in line with the 1979 Joint Economic Report Recommendation No. 12 (p. 25): "The current Federal manpower training programs should be significantly expanded in order to equip unemployed workers with skills to meet entry level requirements." Continuing management training is particularly important in view of the unique responsibility of management for innovation and productivity growth.

RECOMMENDATION FIFTY-THREE

The value of in-house training should be exempt from income taxes.

RECOMMENDATION FIFTY-FOUR

Programs of "executives in residence" in colleges and universities should be expanded, with emphasis on using the expertise of businessmen to develop improvements in management techniques and technological innovations, particularly in the nonteaching functions of the institutions.

RECOMMENDATION FIFTY-FIVE

Leaves of absence for faculty members to work in private enterprises for six months or a year should be encouraged, and programs worked out with business organizations to facilitate such arrangements.

Enhancing health and safety. Investments in maintaining and improving health and safety enhance production and productivity by increasing the length of working life, reducing time lost due to illness or accident, and raising vitality. As is true of education, social returns exceed private pecuniary returns because reasonably good health is a prerequisite to enjoying life as well as to working effectively.

Medical research has been the key to much of the progress in health care. Unfortunately, the pattern of private philanthropy in this area does not generally correspond to the relative incidence and seriousness of various illnesses and debilitating conditions in the population as a whole. Further, the 1962 Amendments to the Pure Food and Drug Act have drastically delayed and reduced the introduction of new drugs, as well as much increasing costs of pharmaceutical research, which has reduced competition in the industry by driving out small firms and discouraging entry.

Of course, the cheapest and most effective way of improving health is by a spread of more healthful life styles with respect to diet, exercise, avoidance of harmful substances, stress management, etc.[34] The schools are the best place to intensify the dissemination of health information, because it is easier to establish healthful patterns of living than it is to change deleterious ones in older people.

34. See Regional Forums on Community Health Promotion, *Promoting Health: Issues and Strategies* (Washington: Department of Health, Education, and Welfare, 1979).

The best plan for ensuring that all Americans have access to adequate medical care is open to debate, but the principle is widely accepted. The important thing is that Congressional proponents of differing approaches agree without further undue delay on effective measures to realize the objective.

RECOMMENDATION FIFTY-SIX

Federal funds for medical research should continue to be expanded and should be directed into areas required to provide balance in allocation of total funds, private and public, in accordance with the relative incidence of various diseases and conditions in the national population.

RECOMMENDATION FIFTY-SEVEN

Congress should relax the requirements for testing new drugs (1962 Amendments to the Pure Food and Drugs Act) in order to achieve a more reasonable balance between safety, costs, and the earlier availability of a wider variety of medical drugs to the public.

RECOMMENDATION FIFTY-EIGHT

The Surgeon General should take the lead in accelerating programs of preventive medicine and disseminating health information to the public, with particular emphasis on providing materials through the schools.

RECOMMENDATION FIFTY-NINE

Advertising of harmful substances should be further restricted and counter-advertising programs expanded.

RECOMMENDATION SIXTY

Congress should liberalize deductions for health care in the individual income tax by lowering the percentage of nondeductible income.

RECOMMENDATION SIXTY-ONE

The Department of Health, Education, and Welfare should devote more resources to the measurement and analysis of productivity in hospitals and other health care facilities, the development of new cost-reducing technologies, and the diffusion of information concerning best practices.

Changes in the labor force mix. Changes in the percentage composition of the employed labor force among groups with differing average rates of compensation affect productivity. As shown in Table 2, after 1966 the bulge in the youthful cohorts, with less experience and productivity as reflected in lower wage rates, had a negative effect on productivity. So, too, did the rising proportion of females, also with less experience on average. The declining labor-force-participation ratios of men over fifty-five years of age, with the greatest experience and average earnings, also contributed to the negative impact.

In general, changes in the labor force mix are not amenable to policy levers. The changes reflect demographic changes and free choices made by individuals—between work and leisure or other pursuits—of which education is the most important for youth. Note also that as the cohort of the post-World War II baby boom moves into ages thirty and over, the changing labor force mix will become positive in the 1980s. Women gaining more experience and moving toward equality of pay with men will also have a positive effect. But there is one area in which policy has had a negative effect and should be changed.

Mandatory retirement ages and the incentives to earlier retirement built into Old Age and Survivors Insurance and into private pension plans have accentuated the trend toward decreasing labor force participation of able workers with valuable experience. Problems may arise in personnel departments in preparing cases for separation or down-grading of older workers who are no longer able to perform their jobs adequately, but such workers generally choose retirement, whereas many more productive workers, particularly in skilled and professional positions, would choose to continue to work if permitted or if incentives to early retirement were reduced.

A slowing of the trend toward earlier retirement is particularly important in view of the projected increases in the proportion of the population over sixty in coming decades, and thus in the dependency ratio and associated burden on the working population to support social security and other pension plans.

RECOMMENDATION SIXTY-TWO

The mandatory retirement age, recently raised from sixty-five to seventy by act of Congress, should be eliminated entirely, as in federal government employment, and incentives to early retirement in the Social Security laws and private pension plans should be reduced.

No attempt is made to spell out specifics, but the recommendation could involve raising the age at which full retirement benefits under OASI would be paid (now sixty-five) or partial benefits paid (now sixty-two), and lowering the age (now seventy-two) at which benefits would be available as a right and not contingent on labor earnings below a certain amount.

Offsets to the declining quality of domestic natural resources

One of the oldest principles of economics is the tendency for diminishing returns to land and other natural resources. As population and production expand in a nation, less productive land is eventually used, the average quality of mineral resources declines, and as resources are exploited more intensively their productivity declines. In the United States, this tendency was much more than offset until the last decade by technological advances in extractive industries. Productivity in farming and mining actually rose substantially faster than in the economy as a whole.[35] Since the late 1960s, however, productivity in agriculture has grown somewhat more slowly, and in the mineral industries it has declined absolutely. Although part of the latter decline resulted from environmental and safety regulations, part reflects the declining average quality of natural resources, particularly oil and gas.

The declining rate of population growth now helps reduce pressures, but the drive for greater energy independence increases them, and they will continue despite occasional temporary reversals that result from significant new discoveries. A number of policies are available to mitigate or at least partially offset the adverse effects of the trend.

RECOMMENDATION SIXTY-THREE

Major reliance should be placed on market pricing of natural resources to promote exploration, conservation in use, and development of substitutes for those resources that are becoming relatively scarce and therefore more expensive.

RECOMMENDATION SIXTY-FOUR

Liberalization of international trade and investment flows must continue to be U.S. policy, buttressed by diplomatic measures to

35. See John W. Kendrick, *Productivity Trends in the United States* (New York: National Bureau of Economic Research, 1961), and (with Elliot Grossman) *Productivity in the United States: Trends and Cycles* (Baltimore: Johns Hopkins University Press, 1979).

try to ensure access to foreign sources of raw materials. This liberalization does not preclude participation in commodity agreements designed to facilitate orderly marketing and to reduce fluctuations in prices through stockpiling arrangements.

RECOMMENDATION SIXTY-FIVE

Efforts of federal agencies, in conjunction with private organizations such as Resources for the Future, to develop long-term projections of resource supply and demand should be strengthened. This strengthening could help the public and private sectors anticipate future price movements and supply problems ahead of pronounced market signals in allocating resources to develop new technologies for mitigating anticipated problems.

RECOMMENDATION SIXTY-SIX

Continued expansion of federal funding for research into new sources of energy and other materials, and to develop new technologies requiring less of the scarcer resources and more efficient production, is necessary.

Facilitating reallocations of labor and capital

In a dynamic economy, continuing changes in demand and supply conditions necessitate relative shifts of labor and capital (including land use) among firms, industries, and geographical areas. In a competitive, market-directed economy, changes in relative prices of outputs and inputs provide the signals and incentives for the reallocations. The relative shifts from uses and industries with lower rates of compensation to those with higher rates help to increase productivity (see Table 2) and effectuate adjustments to technological change.

The problem of facilitating reallocations comprises two elements. The first is the maintenance and enhancement of workable competition so that price signals are not delayed or distorted in product and factor markets. Antitrust laws and actions are our chief reliance in the major part of the private economy, although due consideration must also be given to their effect on technological efficiency and innovation. This trade-off is unavoidable because, although product and process innovations may promote the growth of firm size, they also tend to increase interindustry and product competition and increase the size of the total market so that concentration does not increase in the longer run. In the economic areas of natural monopoly (communications, electric and gas utilities, and most transportation modes), we rely on regulation to simulate the results of market forces. Even in these areas, competition has increased so that greater reliance on market forces is possible; recent literature suggests that regulation could be used more effectively to stimulate innovation and productivity advance.

The other part of the problem lies in the degree of mobility of resources and the speed with which the resources respond to pricing signals. Many of the reallocations are made within existing firms. When labor displacements do occur, traditionally it was left up to the worker to seek and find new employment in expanding sectors. In recent decades, the federal government has assumed greater responsibility for assisting labor adjustments through the Manpower Development and Training Act of 1962 and subsequent amendments that were consolidated and revised in the Comprehensive Employment and Training Act of 1973. This and related legislation, and its administration by the Department of Labor, could doubtless be improved in some respects.

Capital has always been quite mobile, as investors seek to maximize their rates of return. We have already noted, however, the lock-in effect of capital gains taxes. Accelerated depreciation would also promote the relocation of fixed capital. The mobility of both capital and labor is increased by relatively full employment, as is discussed in the next section.

No attempt is made to discuss laws relating to land utilization, but here, too, improvements are possible, although purely economic considerations must be weighed against other values as in all policy formulation.

A final word: despite the seemingly intractable inflation problem, wage and price controls should be enacted only as a temporary last resort for breaking the wage-price spiral. Changes in demand and supply conditions require continued adjustments in product and factor prices, and even a huge price-fixing bureau could not prevent an increasing degree of distortion in relative prices the longer the controls were in effect. One of our great advantages over centralized socialist systems lies in our system of market pricing. We should not sacrifice this advantage lightly.

RECOMMENDATION SIXTY-SEVEN

The antitrust laws should continue to be vigorously enforced, but the Department of Justice should clarify more positively its as-

serted policy of taking into account the prospects for technological innovation and other aspects of national economic policy in evaluating proposed mergers. Further, the antitrust laws should not be interpreted to conflict with the patent regime; and joint R&D ventures should be permitted when there is no collusion regarding markets or pricing.[36]

RECOMMENDATION SIXTY-EIGHT

In considering proposed legislation to require the division of a firm simply because it achieves a certain size or market share, Congress should take into account the possible effects on product and process innovations.

RECOMMENDATION SIXTY-NINE

Market shares resulting principally from the introduction of new technology should not ordinarily be considered in antitrust cases. Proposed "no fault" monopolization legislation that would preclude this consideration would discourage leading firms from promptly introducing new technology and from passing on associated cost savings through price reduction.

RECOMMENDATION SEVENTY

A positive impact on technological advance should be given great weight in cases involving acquisition of small, advanced technology firms by established firms in similar or related fields, unless realistic alternatives are available. The prospect of acquisition is an important incentive to entrepreneurs in organizing technology-based firms, and such acquisitions may hasten the broad-scale implementation of novel technology.

RECOMMENDATION SEVENTY-ONE

Agencies engaged in economic regulations, as for communications, transportation, and power utilities, should permit market prices to play a larger role in promoting efficiency and innovations. Price and entry controls should be eliminated as rapidly as possible, as recently done by the Civil Aeronautics Board. Where necessary, enabling legislation should be amended.

36. See Douglas H. Ginsburg, "Antitrust, Uncertainty and Technological Innovation," a Report to the Panel on the Impact of Antitrust Policies and Practices on Industrial Innovation of the Committee on Technology and International Economic and Trade Issues (Washington: National Academy of Engineering, 1979).

RECOMMENDATION SEVENTY-TWO

Where regulation of natural monopolies is necessary, the rate-making power should be used to promote productivity, as by permitting a return somewhat in excess of the cost of capital for firms that can demonstrate above-average productivity gains.[37] This approach would more closely approximate the result of the competitive market sector, in which above-average profit rates are socially beneficial as a reward and incentive for superior efficiency.

RECOMMENDATION SEVENTY-THREE

Unreasonable restrictions on entry by certain labor unions, professional associations, and other organizations should be eliminated.

RECOMMENDATION SEVENTY-FOUR

Programs to retrain, place, and, where necessary, relocate displaced workers under the Comprehensive Employment and Training Act should be made more effective, and moving allowances increased.[38]

RECOMMENDATION SEVENTY-FIVE

Government intervention to support declining industries or firms should be replaced by a greater emphasis on programs to assist the transfer of resources to expanding industries, as under the Economic Development Act.

RECOMMENDATION SEVENTY-SIX

Expansion and improvement of the federal statistical system is needed to provide more comprehensive and timely data and projections as background for business and governmental decisions in order to assist the process of adjustment to change.

RECOMMENDATION SEVENTY-SEVEN

Wage and price controls should be instituted only as a last resort to break an inflationary spiral, and then only as a temporary expedient.

Volume factors

Growth of the economy and its major industrial divisions opens up opportunities for economies of scale through greater specialization

37. See F. M. Scherer, *Industrial Market Structure and Economic Performance* (Chicago: Rand McNally, 1970).

38. See *Productivity and Job Security: Retraining to Adapt to Technological Change* (Washington: National Center for Productivity and Quality of Working Life, 1977).

of personnel, equipment, and plants and through the spreading of overhead functions over more units. The extent of scale economies varies directly with the rate of economic growth. Thus, acceleration in growth of output as a result of productivity gains promoted by measures of the sort recommended in this paper would reinforce output growth by providing greater scale economies. Note also that several of the earlier recommendations would result in somewhat faster growth of labor and capital inputs, with the same effect.

The rate of economic growth would also be increased by reduced amplitude of economic fluctuations. Since World War II and the passage of the Employment Act of 1946, fluctuations have been of lesser amplitude and duration than was the case before 1946. The 1973–75 contraction, which was more severe than any others since 1937–38, served to remind us that macroeconomic policy formulation must be further refined in order to avoid such contractions in the future. Relatively stable economic growth, by avoiding the dislocations and reduced capital formation that accompany recessions, also serves to enhance the rate of growth compared with what it would be with greater instability. Studies show that industries with greater cyclical fluctuations generally have lower rates of productivity growth, other things equal; and that in periods of greater cyclical instability the business economy as a whole has lower productivity growth than it does in periods of milder fluctuations.[39] Thus, in addition to its other benefits, achievement of steadier economic growth should enhance the rate of growth.

Over the decade 1969–79, the rate of increase in real GNP averaged 2.8 percent a year. For the decade 1980–90, the Bureau of Labor Statistics projects a growth rate of about 3.4 percent, despite a slowing in labor force growth, reflecting somewhat stronger productivity growth as some of the negative forces of the 1970s are reduced or reversed. But no major new policy initiatives are assumed. With initiatives such as those recommended here, the rate of economic growth could exceed 4 percent if serious economic contractions are avoided. This outcome could significantly increase the opportunities for economies of scale in the 1980s compared with the 1970s.

39. See Michael Mohr, "Labor Productivity in the Business Cycle," in John W. Kendrick and Beatrice Vaccara, *New Directives in Productivity Measurement and Analysis* (Chicago: University of Chicago Press for the National Bureau of Economic Research, 1980).

RECOMMENDATION SEVENTY-EIGHT

The staff of the Council of Economic Advisers should be increased to enable the CEA to perform more adequately the function of long- and medium-term projections, and policy formation to achieve more satisfactory rates of growth of productivity, as a centerpiece in achievement of other objectives specified in the Humphrey-Hawkins Full Employment and Balanced Growth Act of 1978—particularly stronger capital formation, reasonable price stability, and improved U.S. competitiveness in world trade.

In the past, the CEA has been largely concerned with short-term stabilization problems with primary emphasis on aggregate demand. Relatively little attention has been paid to policies for attaining longer-term economic objectives, especially supply-side capabilities and incentives. To some extent, the Humphrey-Hawkins Act corrects this imbalance, requiring the CEA to perform its policy analyses within the context of medium-term economic objectives—and to present a program for achieving the goals, although no new program proposals are specifically required.

Despite the Act's provisions, the section of the 1979 CEA report "Economic Objectives and Policy for the Longer Run" is disappointing. Although goals for 1981–83 are set forth, no new policy measures are proposed. As is stated in the 1979 Joint Economic Report under Recommendation No. 40 (p. 41):

> . . . if the targets we establish for the next five years are to be useful, we must have a realistic assessment of the magnitude of probable economic policy changes required to reach those targets. The Council has not provided that assessment, and accordingly we recommend that this requirement of the Employment Act be better observed in the future.

The Council's productivity projection (real GNP per hour) of a 1.5 percent average annual growth rate 1979–83 inclusive, rising to 2.0 percent in 1982–83, seems low, even given the fact that the CEA proposes no policy measures to improve the rate. As the JEC states in its Recommendation No. 24 (p. 59):

> We urge the Administration and Congress to develop specific proposals to stimulate productivity growth. In our view an underlying rate of productivity growth of 1.5 percent per year does not constitute the "adequate productivity growth" called for by the Humphrey-Hawkins Act.

91

To be charitable to the CEA, its insufficient attention to productivity reflects in part an inadequate staff-size, which is the reason for our recommendation. In part, the problem may reflect the 1980 budget restraints on new programs that would increase expenditures or decrease tax receipts perceptibly. Note also that the Administration's National Productivity Council was created in late 1978 and presumably had no input into the CEA report.

RECOMMENDATION SEVENTY-NINE

The Executive Office and the Congress must take the necessary measures to avoid another contraction of the severity of the 1973–75 downturn and, in general, promote reasonably stable economic growth to provide relatively full employment, as called for in the Employment Acts of 1946 and 1978.

Specifics need not be discussed here; however, economic policy analysis has reached the point that the Council of Economic Advisers and other agencies represented on the Economic Policy Group should be able to recommend appropriate policies for achieving reasonable stability to the President. The important thing is that the President, the Congress, and the Federal Reserve Board (to the extent it pursues independent policies) act promptly to put into effect the appropriate fiscal, monetary, incomes, and structural policies.

This is not to suggest that it is possible to "fine-tune" the economy. Fluctuations in rates of growth of a dynamic, predominantly free-enterprise economy will always occur, as will occasional absolute contractions as well. But the contractions can definitely be contained in amplitude and duration by prompt and appropriate policy measures.

Erratic factors may affect productivity changes from year to year, but they have not been large enough to affect longer period rates of change such as are shown in Table 2. For example, weather affects output and productivity, particularly in agriculture and construction. Better weather forecasting, and eventually some form of weather control, would help. Strikes, civil disturbances, and wars are other examples of erratic, essentially unpredictable factors.

Increasing the net contribution of government

Some governmental functions were included in the sets of causal forces already reviewed—economic regulations, taxes, and the use of fiscal policy to promote reasonably steady economic growth. Other functions, mainly of the federal government, should be considered in terms of measures (1) to reinforce positive effects on productivity growth and (2) to reduce negative effects, as shown in Table 2. The positive factors relate chiefly to increasing the productivity of government in rendering the services it provides the private economy, and in promoting the productivity of the business sector. The mitigation of negative impacts relates mainly to the reduction and rationalization of social regulations, although mention is also made of the need for reforms of the welfare system.

Improving productivity-enhancing services and activities. General government purchases, a component of GNP, are made for two major purposes: investments (infrastructure) that benefit the economy, but that the business sector would not generally undertake, and the provision of services to business, and to the public as consumers, that facilitate and supplement the production of enterprises.

The desirability of continued increases in intangible public investments in R&D, education and training, health and safety, and mobility, which help to raise productivity, has already been discussed. The same is true of tangible investments in schools, roads, community facilities, and so on, up to the point at which the expected social rate of return equals the marginal cost of the funds.

The volume and composition of current services should conform at least roughly to the wants of the community; that is what the programming-planning-budgeting system (PPBS) was set up to do, but with indifferent success. The concern here is with the services designed to promote the productivity of the private sector, for which more than $1 billion a year is being spent by the federal government.

A strong focal point within the federal government is needed to provide leadership and coordination of federal programs to promote productivity in the private sector. Following the demise of the National Center for Productivity, its functions were transferred to the Departments of Commerce and Labor and the Office of Personnel Management, and in October 1978 the President established a National Productivity Council (NPC), chaired by the Director of OMB. The NPC, consisting of department and agency heads, meets quarterly and has a staff of only two persons. If this set-up is continued, the staff should be greatly strengthened to enable it to do an effective job. Or, as proposed by C. Jackson Grayson, a new National Productivity Office with adequate authority and funding might be established as part of the Office of the President.[40]

The important thing is that the NPC (or successor organization) not only oversee and coordinate existing programs that directly promote productivity, but that it provide continuing impetus and coordination in policy planning in all of the areas affecting productivity as reviewed in this paper. Close liaison with the concerned agencies (DOE, DOL, OPM, NSF, HEW) would be required, particularly with the CEA and the Economic Policy Group with respect to relevant economic policies. Grayson also proposed that productivity impact statements be prepared by regulatory agencies for major existing programs and significant new regulations and that the Joint Economic Committee hold periodic hearings on productivity programs and policies, as it does on monetary policy. The Council staff could also maintain contact with foreign productivity centers and with the twenty-eight U.S. private sector centers, and encourage the formation of additional private centers to cover all regions of the United States.

In order to track the progress of its productivity improvement efforts, the government needs a more comprehensive set of productivity statistics, now located chiefly in the Bureau of Labor Statistics. A Panel on Productivity Concepts and Measures, set up by the National Academy of Sciences, recently completed a report containing recommendations in this area, which are reflected in the second recommendation below. Expanded and strengthened productivity estimates would also facilitate analysis of productivity trends and relationships and thus serve as a background for projections and policy studies.

RECOMMENDATION EIGHTY

The President should greatly strengthen the staff capabilities of the National Productivity Council, or create a new National Productivity Office, to provide leadership and coordination of federal programs to promote private sector productivity, including a continuing review of the productivity impacts of existing and proposed programs.

RECOMMENDATION EIGHTY-ONE

The Bureau of Labor Statistics should be given funding to expand

40. See Prepared Statement of C. Jackson Grayson, Chairman, American Productivity Center, before the Joint Economic Committee of the United States, February 5, 1979.

and improve its program of productivity statistics and analysis, by major sector and industry of the U.S. economy, with international comparisons, along the lines recommended by the National Research Council's Panel on Productivity Measurement. In addition to improving the basic data, the Bureau should experiment with relating output to nonlabor inputs (capital, energy, and other intermediate products) as well as to labor hours.

The federal government should also increase the productivity of its own operations significantly and help state and local governments do likewise. Thereby, governments can produce more services for the same labor and capital inputs, "more bang for the buck"; or they can provide the same level of services at less cost and reduce the tax burden.

In recent years, the federal government has developed output and productivity measures (published annually by BLS) covering almost two-thirds of its civilian employees. Along with measurement have come efforts to improve productivity. Each year since 1973 the interagency Joint Financial Management Improvement Project has analyzed the productivity data and prepared recommendations for increasing productivity in the several agencies. State and local governments are generally less advanced in productivity measurement and improvement efforts. But a program of the Office of Personnel Management (formerly the Civil Service Commission) provides liaison that could help state and local governments in this field. More generally, federal assistance programs could incorporate incentives for improved productivity, and remove disincentives, in existing and future grants to state and local governments.

RECOMMENDATION EIGHTY-TWO
Support should be increased for the Joint Financial Management Improvement Program in analyzing federal government productivity performance and in preparing and following up on recommendations for improving productivity of the various agencies and functions.

RECOMMENDATION EIGHTY-THREE
The Intergovernment Personnel Program of the Office of Personnel Management should be given the necessary authority and funding to oversee and provide leadership for federal measures to assist

*state and local governments' management improvement and pro-
ductivity enhancement efforts.*[41]

Reducing the negative impacts of government interventions. Ways
of reducing the negative effects of the tax system on saving and investment have already been suggested. Ways the system of welfare
and other transfer payments might be reformed to give greater weight
to the effects on incentives as well as on equity should also be considered. But in this subsection the chief emphasis will be on ways to
reduce the negative effects of social regulations on productivity,
while still pursuing the good objectives regulations were set up to
achieve.

Regulations have slowed innovation and productivity growth in at
least seven ways: (1) diversion of capital expenditures from productive to nonproductive assets; (2) increased costs of product
development; (3) longer product development cycles (as for pharmaceuticals); (4) uncertainties and risks due to changes in standards
on relatively short notice; (5) disproportionate burdening of small
businesses, which results in increased concentration in some industries; (6) growing costs of product liability loss protection and prevention; and (7) excessive reporting requirements. The recommendations below are drawn in part from those set forth by the Advisory
Subcommittee on Environmental, Health, and Safety Regulations of
the Domestic Policy Review Committee.

RECOMMENDATION EIGHTY-FOUR

*The Administration must persevere in its efforts to rationalize the
regulatory process, including implementation of Executive Order
12044 requiring early public involvement before enactment of new
regulations; coordination of agency activities; tightening of procedural requirements for evaluative choices of proposed regulations and for reevaluation of existing regulations; and improvement of evaluation methods. Where regulations are found to have
negative impacts, provisions for minimizing or eliminating such
impacts should be made. Agencies should be held accountable for
the claimed benefits relative to costs and risks. Performance should
be reviewed regularly, and failure to achieve satisfactory results*

41. See Controller General of the United States, *State and Local Government
Productivity Improvement: What is the Federal Role?* (Washington: General
Accounting Office, December 6, 1978).

should be cause for deregulation or substitution of promising alternatives.

RECOMMENDATION EIGHTY-FIVE

Congress should broaden the mandate of the various regulatory agencies to require them to consider the undesirable side-effects of regulatory actions, in particular the effects on innovation, productivity, costs, and product variety. It is particularly important that agencies regulating new product introduction (e.g., FDA regulation of pharmaceuticals) and construction of new plants (EPA) be required to consider the potential effect of their actions on innovation. The agencies might also be required to include in their annual reports specific evaluation of how existing or proposed regulations impact innovation. The Regulatory Council and the Regulative Analysis Review Group should have some members well qualified in the understanding of the process of innovation.

RECOMMENDATION EIGHTY-SIX

Efficiency and innovation would be promoted by greater use of economic incentives (e.g., effluent taxes and fees) to accomplish regulatory goals. The present approach to pollution abatement is prone to uncertainties, delays, and legal proceedings, which would be obviated by the use of effluent fees.[42] The latter approach would provide continuing incentives for the firm to experiment with and develop new antipollution technology to reduce costs.

RECOMMENDATION EIGHTY-SEVEN

The uncertainties of regulation should be decreased and the consistency of regulatory standards and measures increased:

a. Each regulatory agency should issue a statement of long-range regulatory objectives and intent that would serve as a guideline for the regulated parties as well as for agency personnel. The statement should require appropriate notice and consultations with the regulated parties prior to any changes in order to facilitate adjustments to the changes.

b. Whenever two or more agencies are developing policy or regulations on a single issue or interrelated issue, an interagency

42. See Henry G. Grabowski and John M. Vernon, "The Impact of Federal Regulation on Industrial Innovation" (Washington: The National Academy of Engineering, The Committee on Technology and International Economic and Trade Issues, 1979).

coordinating committee should be formed to assure consistency. Likewise, when a single industry or firm has related compliance requirements controlled by two or more laws, consultations within and among agencies should occur to ensure consistency of requirements.

RECOMMENDATION EIGHTY-EIGHT

Regulation should be goal oriented, rather than focusing on means. By regulating standards of performance rather than technology and processes, cost-reducing innovations would be encouraged. Schedules for regulatory compliance must take account of the time required for technological development and the associated investments.

RECOMMENDATION EIGHTY-NINE

In considering and establishing regulatory policies and measures, agencies should be required to study and take account of the impact of their actions on the worldwide competitive position of U.S. industry.

RECOMMENDATION NINETY

Regulatory bodies should try to compensate for the greater relative burdens imposed on small firms by existing and proposed regulations. For example, procedures and paperwork required for compliance should be simplified for smaller-size classes of companies.

RECOMMENDATION NINETY-ONE

Action should be taken to stem the inordinate escalation in product-liability losses. Congress should take the lead by reforming product-liability laws.

RECOMMENDATION NINETY-TWO

The regulatory agencies should confine the scope of regulation with respect both to ends and means within the bounds of existing knowledge. In the meantime, research should be sponsored to develop a better knowledge base, with respect, for example, to the cause-and-effect aspect of health and safety hazards to be regulated, so that more effective regulations can be written.

RECOMMENDATION NINETY-THREE

The recommendations of the Commission on Federal Paperwork should be gradually implemented by the Administration. The

Commission made more than 770 specific recommendations intended to achieve three basic objectives:[43]

a. *A substantial reorganization of government administrative and management machinery that affects the federal paperwork process;*

b. *A new philosophy of service management, so that laws, rules, and regulations are made in a context of true consultation and participation with the people; and*

c. *A continuation and expansion of efforts that have already been mounted by the Administration to cut paperwork. Almost half of the recommendations have been adopted, but implementation of the others could save more than $6 billion of the estimated $100 billion cost to the public of the paperwork burden (which does not include the psychological costs).*

Improving labor efficiency and other factors

The final line of Table 1 is a residual, which we interpret as reflecting primarily the ratio of actual to potential labor efficiency with given technology. It also reflects all the other factors not elsewhere classified, particularly the impacts of changes in values and institutions not measured in the other seven categories.

Ratio of actual to potential labor efficiency. This ratio is the sort of variable revealed by work-measurement studies relating actual to "standard" output of work groups of individuals, based on industrial engineering standards or statistical norms. Its variations reflect changes in worker effort or skill, organizational factors, and possible restrictive work rules or practices.

Much is heard these days concerning a decline in the work ethic and worker discipline, or the lesser value attached to material goals than in earlier times. These are difficult variables to measure. But it is probably true that in jobs where pay is not tied to performance, most people work more or less below their sustainable potential. And University of Michigan surveys show a significant increase in unproductive time at the workplace since the mid-1960s, which partially explains the negative sign of the residual in Table 2.

Against this background, some companies have installed productivity improvement programs, the centerpiece of which is to involve

43. See *Final Summary Report of the Commission on Federal Paperwork* (Washington: October 3, 1977).

workers or their representatives, at all levels in various units of the company, in discussing the ways in which efficiency and productivity can be raised. These are chiefly functional areas where worker input is important, such as job design, reducing defects, improving maintenance of equipment, reducing absenteeism, tardiness, accidents, etc. In some union plants, joint labor-management productivity committees have been established with the same objectives, as in the steel industry beginning with the labor agreement of 1971. Many of the programs, such as the Scanlon plans, involve sharing cost-savings with the workers, or other kinds of incentives.[44] The productivity improvement programs are frequently linked with productivity measurement programs that can be installed as part of broader management information systems. Such programs make it possible to track the progress being made in raising productivity and to identify problem areas, as well as to serve as background for goal-setting, projections, and budgeting.[45] The measures also help raise the productivity consciousness of managers and other employees.

RECOMMENDATION NINETY-FOUR

The Department of Labor should take the lead in assisting firms establish joint labor-management productivity teams or other types of productivity improvement programs. The Department already has an office that promotes labor-management cooperative efforts, whose staff could be expanded. The Federal Mediation and Conciliation Service has also been authorized to promote joint productivity committees and could work with the Department of Labor if funding is secured. The government could enlist the efforts of the private productivity and quality-of-working-life centers, some of which have already been promoting productivity improvement programs in industry.

RECOMMENDATION NINETY-FIVE

The Office of Personnel Management should actively promote the development of productivity committees throughout the federal establishment and provide assistance to state and local governments in establishing similar programs.

44. See William L. Batt, Jr., and Edgar Weinberg, "Labor-Management Cooperation Today," *Harvard Business Review*, January-February 1978, pp. 96–104; and John W. Kendrick, op. cit., Chapter 11.
45. See John W. Kendrick and Daniel Creamer, *Measuring Company Productivity: Handbook With Case Studies*, 2nd edition (New York: The Conference Board, 1965).

RECOMMENDATION NINETY-SIX

Pay and promotion in government agencies should be more closely tied to performance.

RECOMMENDATION NINETY-SEVEN

The U.S. Department of Labor should encourage, and provide assistance in, labor-management negotiations involving the moderation or elimination of restrictive work rules or jurisdictional rules that impair productivity.

Other causal factors. The residual factors are mainly those reflecting changes in values, attitudes, and institutional forms and practices that are not captured by the other variables we have reviewed. Various social indicators show that since the early 1960s there has been a significant increase in negative social trends, such as increasing crime rates, drug use, divorce, social divisiveness, and violent civil disturbances that crested during the Vietnam conflict but still continue sporadically.[46] Although there are data relating to these phenomena, it is difficult or impossible to estimate their influence. Edward F. Denison has estimated that crime has reduced the productivity growth rate by about 0.05 percentage points a year, on average, since 1960.[47] That may seem to be a small figure, but the cumulative property losses and increases in security outlays over two decades are very large. The estimated residual in Table 2 suggests the net effect of these forces has been negative, but no more so in 1973–78 than during the 1948–66 period as a whole, and possibly a bit less negative than during the Vietnam era, 1966–73.

Obviously, measures to reverse negative social tendencies could make a major contribution to productivity growth. But the values, attitudes, and institutions that underlie productivity performance are too vast a subject to be treated here. Note, however, that economists have made quantitative analyses of crime rates and have discovered that crimes against property, in particular, involve an economic calculus: crime rates are lower in jurisdictions where probabilities of apprehension and effective prosecution are higher and penalties are greater than average.

No attempt will be made here to survey the extensive literature on

46. See *Social Indicators,* 1976 (Washington: Bureau of the Census, 1977).
47. Edward F. Denison, "Effects of Selected Changes in the Institutional and Human Environment upon Output per Unit of Input," *Survey of Current Business,* vol. 58 (January 1978), pp. 21–44.

possible reforms of the system of justice in the United States. But two main areas in which the educational system could play a more influential role in helping to reverse some of the negative tendencies of recent years should be examined. The first is "values education," or the teaching of ethics, in the schools, colleges, and professional schools. An increasing number of educators, citizens groups, and school systems see values education as a way to help offset the loosening influence of the family and religious institutions on the young, to combat increasing violence in society and in the schools, and to help youths develop greater social conscience generally. An increasing volume of studies and materials on values education has been developed, and a small but growing number of schools are experimenting with special courses or introducing the content of values education into instructional programs in other areas, such as social studies.

Values education has been defined as "a process of discovering and developing values. Its aim is to encourage teachers and students to raise questions about what constitutes the good life, the good man. It seeks through analysis and survey to discover what people, individually and in groups, believe to be good."[48] There are several major approaches, as described by Edwin Fenton in a paper for a 1977 conference sponsored by the National Institute of Education:[49] (1) values clarification;[50] (2) cognitive moral development;[51] and (3) values analysis.[52]

At the university level, the Carnegie Corporation and the Rockefeller Brothers Fund in 1977 underwrote a study conducted by the Hastings Center, which had already developed programs on medical ethics for medical schools. The final report on "applied ethics" will not be issued until 1980; but, in an article in the September 1979 issue of *Change,* the codirectors David Callahan and Sissela Bok report that

48. Frank B. Brown and Evelyn Tando, *Values Education: Why, What and How?* (Honolulu: University of Hawaii, Department of Education, 1978), p. 10.
49. Edwin Fenton, "The Relationship of Citizenship Education to Values Education," unpublished paper cited in Brown and Tando, Ibid., p. 11.
50. See L. Raths, M. Harwin, and S. Simon, *Values and Teaching,* Second Edition (Columbus: Charles E. Merrill Publ. Co., 1978).
51. The chief exponent of this approach is Lawrence Kohlberg, "Stages of Moral Development as a basis for Moral Education," in C. M. Beck, B. S. Crittenden, and E. U. Sullivan, eds., *Moral Education: Interdisciplinary Approaches* (Toronto: University of Toronto Press, 1971).
52. See Jack R. Fraenkel, *How to Teach About Values: An Analytical Approach* (Englewood Cliffs, N.J.: Prentice-Hall, 1977).

the study will recommend emphatically that the teaching of applied ethics be given a place in the college and professional school curricula.[53] Courses would seek to emphasize that human beings live in a web of moral relationships, that freedom brings responsibilities as well as rights, and that each individual should feel a sense of personal responsibility in making moral choices that bring suffering or happiness to oneself and others. The study estimates that at least 12,000 courses in ethics are now being offered, but there is much room and need for expansion and improvement.

RECOMMENDATION NINETY-EIGHT

The National Institute of Education should encourage and assist school systems at all levels and institutions of higher education to install, expand, and improve instruction and courses in values and ethics.

The second area we are concerned about is the relative ignorance of the majority of Americans with regard to the workings of the economic system, and the need for expansion and improvement of economic education. So many political issues are economic in nature that an informed citizenry is necessary in a democracy to promote legislation conducive to economic efficiency and progress. Beyond that, some knowledge of economics helps people generally understand their roles in the economy and how productive use of their labor and other resources helps promote their own and the general welfare. In particular, an understanding that increases in real income per worker depend basically on raising productivity should have a positive effect on worker attitudes and practices (which ties back to the section on the ratio of actual to potential labor efficiency).

Surveys reveal that most Americans see their role in the economy as passive;[54] they fail to realize that their activities as producers, consumers, and voters make them active participants. Only one person in seven understands the interrelationship of business, labor, and investors in the economy. Workers generally believe that the fruits of increased productivity go to increase profits and dividends, and they think that profit margins are far higher than they actually are. Even

53. See Fred M. Hechinger, "Teaching of Ethics Endorsed," *New York Times*, August 28, 1979.

54. This and the following survey results are cited in the pamphlet, "Economic Illiteracy: Can We Afford it Any Longer?" (New York: Joint Committee on Economic Education, 1979).

more ominous, a recent survey of 21,000 high school students showed that 82 percent do not think competition exists in American business, and 63 percent favored government ownership of enterprises in certain industries (banking, railroads, and steel). As Frederick R. Kappel, former chairman of AT&T said, "If we have enough voters totally ignorant of economic pros and cons, they can vote the country down the drain without even knowing it."[55] U.S. Senate Resolution 316, 89th Congress, stated: "A widespread understanding of the operation and problems of the United States economic system is essential if Americans are to meet their responsibilities as citizens, voters, and participants in a basically private enterprise economy."[56]

The reason for widespread economics "illiteracy" is not hard to find. Less than 20 percent of all Americans have ever taken an economics course. Virtually all colleges offer such courses, but even today only a minority of high school graduates go on to college, and of these a minority takes even one course in economics. Only 27 percent of secondary schools offer an economics course and only 3 percent of all high school students take one. Less than half of the social studies teachers (who are primarily responsible for economics education in the schools) have received any formal training in economics, and the treatment of economics in most social studies textbooks is inadequate.[57]

Yet economics education is being slowly expanded, and a good basis has been built for further expansion, if more resources are forthcoming. The primary organization promoting expansion of the quantity and quality of economics education is the Joint Council on Economic Education, incorporated in 1949.[58] It now has a network of five regional and forty-nine state Affiliated Councils, and more than 190 collegiate Centers for Economic Education. Many other national organizations work with the JCEE. Funding is largely private, from corporations, trade associations, labor unions, farm groups, and some government agencies.

The chief function of the JCEE is to provide school systems, kindergarten through grade 12, with the ways and means of implementing

55. Ibid., p. 1.
56. Ibid., p. 3.
57. See Michael A. MacDowell, "The 'Why' and 'How' of Economic Education," *Educational Perspective,* Journal of the College of Education, University of Hawaii, vol. 17, No. 2, May 1978.
58. This and the following information about the JCEE was largely abstracted from the article by its President, MacDowell, ibid., pp. 3–8.

changes in curriculum to include more economics within existing programs by provision of materials, in-service teacher training, planning, and evaluation at the local level. Intensive summer sessions are held to train teachers in economics, who then train other teachers during the school year. More recently, teachers have been involved in the development of materials. The "Trade-off" series of TV films, with accompanying guides, have been particularly effective.

Complementary to the K–12 program, which now reaches about 10 million students in forty-two states, is the college and university program in more than 170 economics education centers. These centers conduct teacher training programs, provide continuing assistance to schools and community organizations, and conduct extensive research, evaluation, and validity testing of materials, methods, and curricula alternatives. They also maintain resource libraries and distribute materials. At the college level, they try to initiate improvements in the introductory economic principles course.

Recently, the JCEE, in conjunction with the American Economic Association, completed a Master Curriculum Guide in Economics for the Nation's Schools: Part I covers basic concepts that should be mastered by any high school graduate and Part II consists of a series of manuals on the applications of these concepts to specific portions of grades K–3, 4–6, and 7–12. The Council also is involved in citizens' economic workshops, clergy conferences, education-business days, workshops for journalists, and other community projects to promote economic understanding. It helped form a consortium of business, labor, government, and education leaders that established "action committees" to assist teachers in preparing lesson plans, to organize field trips, and to visit classrooms.

The Business Roundtable has called the JCEE "the organization best equipped in its field to reach the objectives we share. The Joint Council appears to be the one national organization which has received widespread recognition for its activities in attempting to improve and increase economic teaching in the schools." There are, however, more than 100 other organizations that attempt to increase economic understanding,[59] although many are specialized in one area or another of the subject, and some seek to promote particular points of

59. See *Organizations Providing Business and Economic Education Information* (Chicago: Public and Government Affairs, Standard Oil Company of Indiana, January 1979).

view, whereas the JCEE attempts to promote an "objective" approach. The various programs have achieved some measurable progress in increasing the scope of economics education and popular understanding. But much remains to be done to reduce the remaining ignorance of economics, including the role of productivity in the economic progress of individuals and of society.

RECOMMENDATION NINETY-NINE

The National Institute of Education, in conjunction with concerned private organizations, should increase support of programs to expand the scope and quality of economic education in the schools, colleges, and the broader community.

In conclusion, it should be underscored that the Joint Council enlists leaders of business, labor, and government to help in the process of economic education. More broadly, everyone has a role in promoting constructive, worthwhile activities and values and in speaking out against destructive, divisive forces. Most of the recommendations in this paper have been addressed to various agencies of government, which is indeed a powerful agent of change. But in the last analysis the rate of productivity growth reflects the health not only of the economy, but of the broader society—its productive and creative forces. Thus, the goal of reversing the productivity slowdown is a challenge to each of us, because society is but the sum of the individuals it comprises.

SUMMARY AND CONCLUDING REMARKS

The discussion that follows is a broad integrative and interpretive summary of the main themes and interrelationships of the topics in the paper. A complete summary outline of the proposed policy options is presented at the end of this paper.

The dominant role of total capital formation in productivity growth stands out in the discussion. According to Table 2, it accounted for three-fourths of the growth of output per unit of labor input in 1948–66, and because the net effect of the other factors was negative, more than all of it after 1966. "Total" capital formation includes not only the conventional tangible investments in structures, equipment, inventories, and natural resources development, but also the "intangible" (nonmaterial) investments in R&D, education and training, health and safety, and mobility. The complementarity of the various types of investment is high. R&D raises rates of return on and demand for the tangible capital goods in which it is embodied, and the tangibles help diffuse new technology. Education prepares the scientists, engineers, and managers who invent and innovate, while technological progress creates demand for more highly educated and trained persons. Better health increases the return on education, and education plays an important role in medical research and in diffusing health information. Mobility is essential for the economy to adapt to and maximize the return on new technology. When one form of investment lags, as has R&D in the past decade, the effectiveness of other types is reduced.

A two-pronged approach was suggested for reaccelerating the growth of the real capital stocks per unit of labor by raising investment rates. First, reasonably steady, predictable, and significant rates of increase in public investments are called for, because governments are a major factor in all types of intangible investment and in new construction, subject to the constraint that expected social rates of return should exceed the marginal cost of funds. Second, various tax and other incentives were proposed to spur private business and personal investments in these areas. The preferred vehicles for business tangible fixed investments were accelerated depreciation (possibly the 10-5-3 formula of the Jones-Conable bill); further reduction of the capital gains tax at least back to the pre-1969 25 percent maximum; and a reduction in the double taxation of dividends, on either a paid or received basis, or some of both. The suggested approach for business R&D is to blanket R&D under the 10 percent investment tax credit or to employ a larger incremental investment tax credit that might have greater effect per dollar of taxes foregone. An increase in student aid programs was proposed for individual education and training outlays, including an expanded loan or loan-guarantee program and income tax deductions. The latter approach was also suggested, with more liberal provisions than at present, for health outlays, and it could also be applied to moving expenses to facilitate labor mobility.

At relatively high employment, measures to increase saving would be needed to permit noninflationary further expansion of investments and to help hold down interest rates. Several selective ways of providing incentives for personal saving were offered, short of exempting all saving from personal income taxes, which presents computational and administrative difficulties. The measures proposed to increase after-tax profits also increase business saving. And governmental surpluses in times of prosperity add to the private saving pool as a source of finance.

Measures to accelerate productivity and reduce relative prices of capital goods stimulate investment. The same holds true of capital services, and for each of these areas measures were proposed for increasing relevant R&D and promoting cost-reducing technology in order to increase intangible investments. A supplemental investment tax credit was one means proposed. Sector productivity committees might be formed, including business and academic representatives, to develop other ways of promoting technological advance to cut costs and improve quality in R&D, education, and health care, as well as in the equipment and construction industries. Reducing restrictive work rules and practices, modernizing building codes, and rationalizing regulations are particularly important in construction.

Another theme was reliance on the market pricing system. Vigorous enforcement of antitrust laws was supported, although with a proviso that due regard should be paid to effects on innovation that might do more to reduce prices in the long run than would the immediate antimerger action. The forces of competition can be relied on to supplement economic regulation to a greater extent than in the past. In particular, market pricing is favored as a means of coping with natural resource problems as rising relative prices of oil and gas provide incentives for conservation in use and for search and research to increase production and productivity. Protection of particular companies or industries from domestic and legitimate foreign competition is not favored, except for urgent national security considerations. But government assistance to displaced labor for retraining and relocation seems equitable—the costs of productivity advance, which benefits the community at large, should not fall on individuals who are displaced through no fault of their own. The main problem with the Employment and Training Administration seems to be lack of administrative competence.

Special measures to help technology-based small companies can be justified on an "infant firm" argument, which parallels the infant industry argument for temporary protection until the firms and industries are viable competitively. Also, some of the assistance is designed merely to offset regulatory costs that fall disproportionately on small firms.

It should be emphasized that the proposed tax measures are designed primarily to offset the anti-saving/investment bias of the present tax system. That is, people would save and invest more if government did not reduce rates of return to savers and investors through income and related taxes. A major argument for VAT is its neutrality in this regard.

The various policy directions may suggest some ambivalence toward the role of governments, but that is not the case. The recommendations recognize the legitimate functions of government and advocate only that those functions be performed more effectively and efficiently, which means accentuating the positive and minimizing the negative. In addition to proposals for mitigating negative impacts of taxes, a host of specific recommendations were made for reform of both economic and social regulations to reduce their unfavorable impact on productivity while still seeking to effectuate their socially mandated objectives. Although some trade-offs may be necessary, we believe they can be tilted more in favor of the productivity goal; in fact, momentum in this direction is now strong within the federal establishment.

In accentuating the positive, governments can certainly increase the productivity with which they use resources to provide services to the community. The federal government should establish a strong National Productivity Office to provide leadership and coordination among federal agencies to develop and execute the kinds of policies proposed in this paper. The productivity impacts of public programs must be subjected to continuing review, and a continuing effort should be maintained to improve institutional arrangements and practices and devise new policy measures to promote productivity advance. Long-range projection and policy planning are as necessary for governments as they are for private corporations, but planning should liberate and stimulate the productive and creative powers of individuals, not control them.

With respect to values and attitudes, education can do a better job in promoting understanding of our social and economic system so that individuals can function more effectively and, as citizens, can help produce and facilitate the institutional changes that are inevitable in a dynamic setting of rapid technological change. In the area of work attitudes and labor efficiency in the short run, the Department of Labor, in conjunction with the twenty-eight private sector productivity centers, should promote and assist in the organization of joint labor-management productivity teams or other types of productivity improvement programs in firms, governmental units, and private nonprofit institutions. By involving labor at all levels in developing ways to increase efficiency, and by enhancing "productivity-mindedness," these efforts have had some dramatic successes in the past (as have the Japanese "quality circles"). Further, productivity committees for industries and other sectors can be useful in dealing with broader issues, such as business-government relations.

Most persons and groups could probably agree on the general nature and thrust of most of the policy initiatives proposed in this paper. There will undoubtedly be disagreement with some of the specific tax reform and expenditure proposals, especially the idea of using a value-added tax as a means of recouping revenue losses from reduction of income taxes. But the increases in aggregate supply and demand that would result from a program of the sort proposed here would increase tax revenues from existing sources sufficiently to make up much of the initial reduction in revenue from the recommended tax cuts. Of course, a productivity-enhancing program of legislation would have to be phased in gradually as economic, budgetary, and political conditions permit. That is why priority should be given to strengthening the National Council on Productivity or to creating a new productivity organization in the Executive Offices of the President—to help plan the strategy for implementing the productivity promotion program that was agreed on.

The purpose of this paper has been to present a broad menu of policy options, rather than to suggest specific policy measures on which business and higher education could agree and on which joint action might be taken. Such measures would have to emerge from joint discussions for which this paper and others will serve as a background. But some general comments can be made in this area of special concern to the Forum.

Tax measures to stimulate private investment are obviously of chiefly academic interest to representatives of public and private nonprofit education institutions, although higher education would support the creation of a favorable investment climate as a precondition for a healthy growing economy that benefits all sectors. But both business and education have an immediate interest in measures to increase R&D and promote technological growth. A federal policy of significant annual increases in real R&D funding, both basic and applied, clearly would benefit both groups. So would tax incentives for corporate research grants to universities. And both groups would find common ground in arrangements for joint applied research in university centers, such as proposed by Senator Stevenson in S. 1250.

University research personnel and companies would both benefit from the assignment of patent rights from government-funded R&D. Both would benefit from the several recommendations to expand the dissemination of scientific and technological information, including that from foreign sources. Both should cooperate with government procurement policies designed to stimulate innovation (though it might be uncomfortable), and each might consider using innovative procurement policy on its own suppliers.

The proposals to strengthen the educational system, particularly higher education, with respect to efficiency, quality, and accessibility, are of concern to business, which is interested in an adequate supply of trained manpower to meet its growth needs. Business input on future labor requirements, and possibilities of applying industrial technologies to higher education, could be valuable, possibly through advisory committees or expansion of executive-in-residence programs. Reciprocal scholar-in-residence programs of companies could also be of mutual value by bringing a somewhat different set of skills and viewpoints into firms and by increasing the understanding of academics as to how business operates, particularly in economics, engineering, and business administration. The Forum could work out some concrete arrangements in this area.

The interest of business in the financing of education is somewhat academic, but like the academics' interest in private investment, the business sector obviously has a stake in the continued health of the educational system.

The two groups share with all groups and individuals a vital interest in improving the health of the nation. They are both in a position to help in the dissemination of health information, and certain companies and universities play a key role in medical and related research.

Views will differ in all sectors as to the desirability of lifting mandatory retirement ceilings and decreasing incentives to early retirement. But as the work force becomes more skilled and professional, all sectors can benefit from retaining their most experienced employees who are willing and able to continue to work.

With respect to reallocations and labor and capital mobility, the market system can be usefully supplemented by socioeconomic projections and futures research. The skills and knowledge of both academic and business people are needed in this area. The Forum might well consider ways of promoting research on the future, and the offering of courses or seminars for both business and university administrators and others to help alert them to developing trends to consider in planning.

Regarding the role of government, both business and education have been adversely affected by regulations and the associated paper work burden. Both groups can find common ground in recommending reductions and rationalization in this area. As to the positive role of government, all sectors benefit from macroeconomic policies to promote strong and relatively stable economic growth and, if possible, a reduction of inflation by measures short of price controls. Like all sectors, both business and education could benefit from a strong federal productivity organization that would promote on a continuing basis the kinds of policies proposed here. They could both contribute importantly to advisory committees that would presumably be convened by the National Productivity Organization. In fact, the Forum might consider working out a specific plan for such an organization to present to the President and the appropriate congressional committees.

Productivity improvement programs are already spreading in industry. There is no reason why education institutions should not institute such programs within their various functional areas, including teaching.

Economics education is already a function of the schools and colleges; the problem is to improve and expand it. Businessmen already have an input in this area, as noted in the description of JCEE programs, but it could be expanded and more firms could make introductory economic instruction available to their employees who have not had it and want it.

In short, there is no dearth of ways in which business and education can act separately and together to improve productivity. The important thing is to step up the action!

Summary of Proposed Policy Options

Note: This outline should be used in conjunction with the discussions in the paper, which provide background and fuller explanations. Page references to the text are given after each major subheading.

Stimulating business investment and saving (p. 54)

Improving the investment climate (p. 56)
1. Measures to enhance business confidence:
    a. Promote productivity growth by combination of policies recommended in this paper, thus contributing to reduced inflation
    b. Reduce instability of economic growth
    c. Rationalize government regulations and other intervention in economy

Increasing returns on investments (p. 57)
2. Restore adequate profit margins after adjustment for inflation
3. Reduce average unit cost increases relative to average price increases
4. Reduce average effective tax-rate on corporate profits by one or more of the following measures:
    a. Increase depreciation allowances
        1) Shorten lives of assets in computing tax-depreciation (as in 10-5-3 Jones-Conable bill formula)
        2) Index depreciation to replacement cost
    b. Increase the investment tax credit and expand its coverage to new construction
    c. Reduce the corporate income tax rate
    d. Reduce or eliminate the double taxation of dividends by partial or complete deductibility of dividends from the corporate profits tax base
    e. Give further study to integration of the personal and corporate income taxes
5. Reduce personal income tax rate
    a. Reduce rates on all brackets, and/or index the brackets
    b. Reduce the 70 percent tax marginal rate on "unearned," property income to the 50 percent tax rate that applies to labor income

Reducing the explicit or implicit cost of financing new investment (p. 61)
6. Measures to raise equity prices and reduce the cost of equity financing

113

7. More favorable tax treatment of capital gains
   a. "Rollover" provision to exempt capital gains that are reinvested
   b. Reduce or eliminate capital gains tax
   c. Tax only the part of capital gains which exceeds the increase in the CPI over the holding period
   d. Liberalize loss deduction provisions
8. Reduce the double taxation of dividends by increasing the $100 dividend exclusion, or by partial credits against dividends received
9. Reduce the real interest rate by encouraging saving by measures in addition to recommendations 2–5.
10. Eliminate Regulation Q
11. Reduce the rate of taxation on interest by exempting some amount or proportion, or taxing only *real* interest receipts
12. Expand savings plans, such as IRA and Keogh, on which taxes are deferred; and expand tax exemption or deferral on income from property, e.g., dividend reinvestment
13. Plan governmental budget surpluses at high employment by curbing expenditure increases

Value-added tax (p. 64)
14. Consider and study value-added tax as means of recouping initial tax losses from income tax reductions

Accelerating relative productivity growth and relative price reductions in capital goods industries (p. 65)
15. A higher investment tax credit for capital goods manufacturers than for other firms
16. Priority for these producers in other applicable measures to promote cost-reducing innovations

Promoting advances in technological knowledge and innovation (p. 66)

Policies to increase R&D activities (p. 66)
17. Federal funding of basic and applied R&D should be gradually and predictably increased in real terms
18. Expand the present investment tax credit to cover business-financed R&D, (or)
19. Grant a larger tax credit on annual increments in R&D outlays
20. Expand the present tax credit to include laboratory construction, and consider expensing both lab equipment and plant for tax purposes, in lieu of investment tax credits for business
21. Grant R&D subsidies of 10 percent for firms with no net income, and consider subsidies as a substitute for the tax credit generally

22. Establish a federal government organization to support cooperative business-university R&D projects, along the lines of S. 1250

Revising the patent system to promote invention and innovation (p. 69)
23. Lengthen the period of patent protection
    a. Increase from 17 to 20 years, or
    b. Extend to compensate for delays in commercialization due to regulations
24. Transfer patent rights made under government contract or funding to firms or individuals responsible
25. Improve the reliability of the patent grant:
    a. Strengthen the Patent and Trademark Office to provide modern search tools and rigorous examinations of applications
    b. Provide a reexamination process
    c. Provide a central court to hear patent appeals
26. Require federal courts to conduct patent litigations with express concern for time and expense
27. The statutory standard of patentability should be clarified
28. Encourage other countries to provide U.S. inventors the right to obtain enforceable patents

Expanding the dissemination of scientific and technological information (p. 71)
29. The Patent and Trademark Office should strengthen its information gathering, retrieval, and dissemination functions
30. The Worldwide Information and Trade System in the Commerce Department should be strengthened, and collect information about foreign regulations, standards, and requirements for product approval
31. The federal government should augment its efforts to increase international technology transfer by further negotiations
32. The informational program of the Office of Technology Assessment and Forecast of the PTO should be expanded with respect to foreign technologies
33. More technical information should be made available by federal agencies

Using procurement policies to promote innovation (p. 73)
34. The Office of Federal Procurement Policy (OFP) should issue and execute a policy statement that establishes goals and methods for stimulating innovation
35. Contracting personnel in GSA should be made more aware of technological developments in their fields
36. The OFP should share its developing expertise on use of procurement policy to stimulate product and cost-reducing innovations by sup-

pliers with state and local governments, including school systems and universities

Promoting small technology-based enterprises (p. 75)

37. Allow more favorable stock-options for founders and key personnel
38. Allow tax-free rollover of equity investments, and the flow-through to investors of start-up losses
39. Simplify SEC Rule 146 and liberalize Regulation A limits
40. Aid by procurement policy and assistance with regulatory compliance
41. Expand SBA direct loans and its financial assistance to small business investment companies

Increasing the quality of labor (p. 76)

Policies to promote the quantity and quality of education and training per worker (p. 76)

42. The National Institute of Education should expand its support for research on and development of new and improved educational methods and technologies
43. The NIE should promote the diffusion of new, tested technologies, encouraging centralized purchasing consortia
44. Colleges and universities should require courses in education, including usage of modern technologies, or prospective and current faculty members
45. Increase funding of federal student aid programs, and relax aid requirements in some instances
46. Institute tax credits for some portion of tuition payments
47. Expand funding or government guarantees of student loans
48. Place greater emphasis on aptitude and interest testing and career counseling
49. Expand continuing adult education programs, including the "open university"
50. The NSF should steadily increase research grants to higher education institutions
51. The federal government should provide tax credits or matching grants for business or individual contributions for basic and applied research at public and private nonprofit institutions
52. Expand and strengthen formal and on-the-job training programs authorized under CETA
53. The value of in-house training must remain exempt from income taxes
54. Expand "executive-in-residence" programs of higher education institutions, and utilize executives to improve nonteaching technologies and methods
55. Expand "scholar-in-residence" programs of companies

Enhancing health and safety (p. 82)

56. Expand federal funds for medical research, and improve the allocational balance in relation to requirements
57. Relax testing requirements of the 1962 Amendments to the Pure Food and Drug Act
58. Accelerate programs of preventive medicine and dissemination of health information, with particular emphasis on the schools
59. Further restrict advertising of harmful substances, and step-up counter-advertising
60. Liberalize deductions for health care in the individual income tax
61. The Department of HEW should devote more resources to measurement and analysis of productivity in hospitals and other health facilities, developing new technologies, and promoting diffusion of best practices

Changes in labor force mix (p. 83)

62. Mandatory retirement age requirements should be abolished, and incentives for early retirement under Social Security and private pension plans reduced

Offsets to the declining quality of domestic natural resources (p. 85)

63. Rely primarily on market pricing to promote exploration, conservation, and development of substitutes
64. Liberalize international trade and investment flows, buttressed by diplomatic measures to ensure access and to combat cartel pricing
65. Improve long-term demand and supply projections to help anticipate market signals
66. Continue federal funding of research into new sources and new technologies

Facilitating reallocations of labor and capital (p. 86)

67. The antitrust laws must continue to be enforced vigorously, but with due consideration of impacts on innovation
    a. Antitrust laws should not be interpreted to conflict with the patent regime
    b. Joint R&D ventures should be permitted
    c. In reviewing proposed mergers, weight should be given to innovational effects
68. In considering proposed legislation to break up certain classes of firms, Congress should consider the effect on innovational activity as well as on markets
69. Increased market shares resulting from the introduction of new technology should not ordinarily lead to antitrust suits

117

70. Acquisition of small technology-based firms by larger firms should generally be permitted
71. Economic regulations should accord a larger role to market forces, as in the airline industry, and entry controls should be eliminated
72. Public utility commissions should use the rate-setting power more fully to promote productivity growth
73. Unreasonable restrictions on entry by some labor unions and professional associations should be abolished
74. CETA programs to retrain, place, and relocate displaced workers should be expanded and made more effective
75. Government intervention to support declining firms and industries should be replaced by more assistance for the transfer of resources to expanding sectors, as under the Economic Development Act
76. Expand and improve the federal statistical system to provide more timely data, analysis, and projections
77. Wage and price controls should be instituted only as a last resort to break an inflationary spiral, and then only on a temporary basis

Volume factors (p. 89)

78. The staff of the Council of Economic Advisers should be expanded to enable it to perform more adequately the function of medium- and long-term projects and policy formulation to achieve stronger rates of economic growth
79. The Economic Policy Group and the Congress must take the necessary measures to mitigate economic contractions generally, and to prevent the current slow-down from reaching the proportions of the 1973–75 contraction

Increasing the net contribution of government (p. 92)

Improving productivity-enhancing services and activities (p. 93)
80. The President should create a National Productivity Office to provide leadership and coordination of federal programs to promote productivity
81. The Bureau of Labor Statistics should expand its productivity statistics and analysis program
82. Expand the Joint Financial Management Improvement Program for analyzing federal government productivity performance and making and following-up on recommendations for improving productivity of the agencies
83. The Intergovernmental Personnel Program of the Office of Personnel Management should be given the necessary funding to assist state and local government management improvement and innovation efforts

Reducing the negative impacts of government interventions (p. 96)

84. The Administration must implement more fully Executive Order 12044 which directs reforms of the regulatory system
85. Congress should broaden the mandates of regulatory agencies, requiring them to consider the undesirable side-effects of regulatory actions, particularly as they inhibit and delay innovation
86. Use economic incentives (e.g., effluent taxes) to accomplish regulatory goals
87. The uncertainties of regulation should be decreased, and consistency increased:
    a. Issue statements of long-range regulatory objectives and intent to serve as guidelines, and consult with regulated parties prior to changes in regulations
    b. Establish interagency coordinating committees to ensure consistency of regulations
88. Regulate standards of performance rather than technology and processes
89. Regulatory agencies should take account of impacts of their actions on U.S. competitiveness in world trade
90. Procedures and paperwork should be simplified for smaller companies
91. Product liability laws should be reformed
92. Regulations should be confined within the bounds of existing knowledge, and the relevant knowledge-base expanded
93. The recommendations of the Commission on Federal Paperwork should be further implemented to reduce the paperwork burden

Improving labor efficiency and other factors (p. 99)

Increasing the ratio of actual to potential labor efficiency (p. 99)

94. The Department of Labor, in cooperation with private productivity centers, should encourage and assist firms to establish joint labor-management productivity teams or other types of productivity improvement programs
95. The Office of Personnel Management should promote the establishment of productivity committees in federal agencies, and assist this activity in state and local governments
96. Pay and promotion in government agencies should be more closely tied to performance
97. Restrictive work rules should be moderated or eliminated

Other causal factors (p. 101)

98. The National Institute of Education should encourage school systems and higher education institutions to install, expand, and improve instruction and courses in values and ethics

99. Expand the scope and quality of economic education in the schools, colleges, and in the broader community

Addendum A

PRODUCTIVITY POLICY INTERESTS OF BUSINESS AND HIGHER EDUCATION

Although this paper does not address specific policy measures that business and academic leaders could pursue, there are many areas of common interest. For example, tax measures to stimulate private investment are obviously of chiefly academic interest to representatives of public and private nonprofit educational institutions, although we would support the creation of a favorable investment climate as a precondition for a healthy growing economy that benefits all sectors. But both business and education have an immediate interest in measures to increase R&D and promote technological advance. A federal policy of significant annual increases in real R&D funding, both basic and applied, clearly would benefit both sectors. So would tax incentives for corporate research grants to universities, and both sectors would find common ground in arrangements for joint applied research in university centers, such as proposed by Senator Stevenson in S. 1250.

University research personnel and companies would both benefit from the assignment of patent rights from government-funded R&D. Both would benefit from the several recommendations to expand the dissemination of scientific and technological information, including that from foreign sources. Both sectors should cooperate with government procurement policies designed to stimulate innovation (though it might be uncomfortable), and each might consider using innovative procurement policy on its own suppliers.

The proposals to strengthen the educational system, particularly higher education, with respect to efficiency, quality, and accessibility are of concern to business with its interest in an adequate supply of trained manpower to meet its growth needs. Business input with respect to future labor requirements, and possibilities of applying industrial technologies to the educational sector, could be valuable, possibly through advisory committees or expansion of executive-in-residence programs. Reciprocal scholar-in-residence programs of companies could also be of mutual value by bringing a somewhat different set of skills and viewpoints into firms and by increasing the understanding of academics as to how business operates, particularly in economics, engineering, and business administration. This is an area in which the Forum could work out some concrete arrangements.

The interest of business in the financing of education is somewhat academic, but like the academics' interest in private investment, the business sector obviously has a stake in the continued health of the educational system.

The two sectors share with all groups and individuals a vital interest in improving the health of the nation. They are both in a position to help in the dissemination of health information, and certain companies and universities play a key role in medical and related research.

Views will differ in all sectors as to the desirability of lifting mandatory retirement ceilings and decreasing incentives to early retirement. But as the work force becomes more skilled and professional, all sectors can benefit from retaining their most experienced employees who are willing and able to continue to work.

With respect to reallocations and labor and capital mobility, the market system can be usefully supplemented by socioeconomic projections and futures research. The skills and knowledge of both academic and business people are needed in this area. The Forum might well consider ways of promoting research on the future, and the offering of courses or seminars for both business and university administrators and others to help alert them to developing trends to consider in planning.

Regarding the role of government, both business and education have been adversely affected by regulations and the associated paper work burden. Both sectors can find common ground in recommending reductions and rationalization in this area. As to the positive role of government, all sectors benefit from macroeconomic policies to promote strong and relatively stable economic growth and, if possible, a reduction of inflation by measures short of price controls. Like all sectors, both business and education could benefit from a strong federal productivity organization that would promote on a continuing basis the kinds of policies proposed here. They could both contribute

121

importantly to advisory committees that would presumably be convened by the National Productivity Organization. In fact, the Forum might consider working out a specific plan for such an organization to present to the President and the appropriate congressional committees.

Productivity improvement programs are already spreading in industry. There is no reason why educational institutions should not institute such programs within their various functional areas, including teaching.

Economic education is already a function of the schools and colleges; the problem is to improve and expand it. Businessmen already have an input in this area, as noted in the description of JCEE programs, but it could be expanded and more firms could make introductory economic instruction available to their employees who had not had it and want it.

In short, there is no dearth of ways in which business and education can act separately and together to improve productivity. The important thing is to step up the action!

Addendum B

THE PRESIDENT'S INDUSTRIAL INNOVATION
INITIATIVES OF OCTOBER 31, 1979

On October 31, 1979 (subsequent to preparation of this paper), the President transmitted a message to the Congress, and the White House issued a companion fact sheet, on "The President's Industrial Innovation Initiatives." The various initiatives were presented under nine major headings, as reproduced below. The initiatives were selected from the recommendations contained in the task force reports made in connection with the "Domestic Policy Review" begun in April 1978. Because most of those recommendations were included in this paper, the President's initiatives are largely paralleled there, with a few exceptions or modifications. Note also that the new initiatives do not include tax measures—the Administration is presumably waiting until the budgetary and economic situation is more propitious. A brief commentary follows the summary of the President's initiatives.

SUMMARY FROM THE FACT SHEET

Enhancing the transfer of information

Scientific and technical information is created largely by universities, government laboratories, industrial laboratories and by similar activities abroad. It becomes the knowledge needed in industrial innovation when it is relevant to industry's problems or opportunities and when it is effectively transferred to the industry user. New actions deal with improving the transfer of existing, potentially relevant information; and improving the rate at which we create such information. To facilitate the transfer of existing information, the President is taking action in two areas.

1. *The NTIS Center for Utilizing Federal Technology*

The Federal government annually undertakes approximately $10 billion of R&D at Federal laboratories and Federally-funded R&D Centers. The National Technical Information Service (NTIS) provides a channel of communication with industry concerning these research results. It has a broad understanding of industry needs, and Federal laboratory activity. It is in position to help inform industries of technological opportunities of which they might otherwise be uninformed.

The President has decided to enhance the NTIS program by creation of a Center in NTIS with the mission of improving the flow of knowledge from Federal laboratories and R&D Centers to industries outside the mission agencies' purview. The FY 1981 cost of the program will be $1.2 million and subsequent year costs will not exceed $2 million per year.

2. *Foreign Technology Utilization*

Foreign technological and scientific advances are an untapped source of technological information for American innovation. An inadequate ability exists within the Federal government and within industries to gather, analyze, organize, and disseminate information regarding foreign research and development activities that bear on the competitiveness of U.S. industry. Other countries gather such information on the U.S.

a. The President has decided to have the NTIS include extensive foreign technical literature collection and translation in its present activities. This move will make relevant foreign literature available to industry. The first year program cost will be $1.8 million.

b. The President intends to have the Departments of State and Commerce interview volunteer returning U.S. overseas visitors about observed foreign technological developments, collect reports from our science counselors, and collect photographs, and other unpublished information. This information will be merged with the NTIS data base on foreign technical literature to make it widely and easily available to industry. The 1981 cost of this program will be $2.4 million.

Increasing technical knowledge

The Federal government supports a broad range of R&D activities from basic through applied research, development and demonstration in areas of interest to industry. Most of this work is to meet some specific social or national need, as in the case of future development or defense, or to provide a foundation for future advance, as in the case of basic research. Unlike many foreign countries the U.S. does not make major direct governmental investments in the development of technologies. The President will take actions in three areas aimed at enhancing the technical knowledge base in the United States.

1. *Generic Technology Centers*

The President believes there is a Federal role in the development of generic technologies—that is, technologies that underlie industrial sectors. Examples include welding and joining, robotics (automated assembly) corrosion prevention and control, non-destructive testing and performance monitoring and tribology (science of lubricants). Because the benefit from advances in generic technology to any one firm (or even one industrial sector) may be small, there is less investment in the development of generic technologies than would be justified by the benefits that flow from these activities.

The President has decided to establish non-profit centers—at universities or other private sector sites—to develop and transfer generic technologies. Each of the centers will be targeted on a technology that is involved in the processes of several industrial sectors, and has the potential for significant technological upgrading. It would not supplant efforts in the private sector that are designed for specific product development.

- Each center will be jointly financed by industry and government, with the government's share dropping to 20 percent or less of the center's cost in the fifth year.
- Four centers will be established in FY 81 at a cost of $6–8 million. Three will be sponsored by the Department of Commerce and one by the National Science Foundation.
- In future years, the size of the program will depend on the proposals received, and the experience gained from this initial effort.

2. *Regulatory Technology Development*

One major cause of the modification of industrial processes in recent years has been the obligation to assure compliance with environmental, health or safety regulation. Innovation is important in making these changes so that the new processes meet regulatory objectives at the least cost. Federal investment in the development of compliance technology already is substantial. There are very large Federal expenditures on technologies for the clean burning of coal or to improve the safety of mines. But there are instances in which the affected sector is unable to perform the work or to assure speedier compliance than the market can provide.

The President will ask the Office of Management and Budget, in the course of its crosscut of regulatory activities in developing the FY 81 budget, to examine closely the nature and extent of expenditures on compliance technology and to bolster the Federal effort.

3. *Improved Industry-University Cooperation in R&D*

The scientific and technological strength of American universities has not been harnessed effectively in promoting industrial technological advance. In order to achieve this end, in FY 1978 the NSF established a program for the support of high quality R&D projects that are proposed jointly by industry-university research teams.

a. The President has decided to provide $20 million of new funds at NSF in FY 1981 for this purpose with subsequent year support at a similar level.

b. In addition, the President plans to extend the NSF program to other agencies. NSF will work with DOD, DOE, EPA, and NASA in FY 1980 and with other agencies in subsequent years to initiate such university-industry cooperative R&D programs and to establish quality-control procedures as effective as the NSF peer review system. Each agency will formulate plans for building its support for this program with the objective of reaching an aggregate of $150 million.

Strengthening the patent system

Patents serve several important functions in the innovation process. First, they provide an inventor with an incentive—a monopoly limited in time. Second, the exclusive rights provided by a patent can stimulate a firm to make the often risky investment that is required to bring an invention to market. Finally, a patent provides an important method for disclosure of information about inventions and their uses to the public.

1. *Uniform Government Patent Policy*

The Policy Review identified strong arguments that the public should have an unrestricted right to use patents arising from Federal sponsorship.

These patents were derived from public funds and all the public have an equitable claim to the fruits of their tax dollars. Moreover, exclusive rights establish a monopoly—albeit one limited in time—and this is an outcome not favored in our economy.

Several competing considerations, however, urge that exclusive rights to such patents should be available. First, government ownership with the offer of unrestricted public use has resulted in almost no commercial application of Federal inventions. Without exclusive rights, investors are unwilling to take the risk of developing a Federal invention and creating a market for it. Thus, ironically, free public right to use patents results, in practical terms, in a denial of the opportunity to use the invention. Second, many contractors, particularly those with strong background and experience with patents, are unwilling to undertake work leading to freely available patents because this would compromise their proprietary position. Thus, some of the most capable performers will not undertake the government work for which they are best suited.

As a result of the strength of these considerations, most agencies have the authority in some circumstances to provide exclusive rights. But because of the difficulty of balancing the competing considerations, this issue has been unsettled for over 30 years and the various agencies operate under different and contradictory statutory guidance. The uncertainty and lack of uniformity in policy has itself had a negative effect on the commercialization of technologies developed with Federal support. As a result, there is an active interest in the Congress and among the agencies to establish a clear and consistent policy.

The President considered a range of options, from always vesting title in the contractor, to maintaining the status quo. In arriving at his decision, the President considered the following factors:

- *Uniformity.* The agencies are currently governed either by an array of different statutes or, in the absence of statute, by Presidential guidance. Indeed, some agencies have different statutory guidance on patents governing different programs. In light of this, there is substantial confusion among contractors who perform R&D for several agencies or programs.
- *Impact on innovation.* Exclusive rights to a patent may be necessary to ensure that a firm will make the often risky investment that is required to bring an invention into production and to develop a market for it. Exclusive rights provide protection from other firms that might skim the profit from the market by copying the invention after the risk and cost of introduction are reduced by the first firm's efforts.
- *Administrative burden.* Any policy that requires an agency to make decisions imposes some administrative costs.
- *Uncertainty.* A clear and easy-to-apply rule is preferable to an ambig-

uous rule for the guidance it offers to both industry and government officials.

- *Contractor participation in government programs.* Firms with strong proprietary positions are unwilling to accept government contracts that would result in freely available patents.
- *Competition.* Exclusive rights foreclose competition in the marketing of the invention covered by the patent and serve, in some cases, to enhance the recipient's market power.

a. The President has decided to seek legislation that would establish a *uniform* government policy with exclusive licenses in the field of use. Title to the patent will be retained by the Government, but the contractor will obtain exclusive licenses in fields of use that he chooses to specify and in which he agrees to commercialize the invention. There will be an exception where the agency determines that such a license would be inconsistent with either the agency mission or the public interest. In most cases, the allocation would be after the invention has been identified, rather than at the time of contracting. The Government would license in all fields of use other than those claimed by the contractor. The Government would retain march-in rights that can be exercised in the event the licensee does not develop the patent.

b. The President also supports the retention of patent ownership by small businesses and universities, the prime thrust of legislation now in the Congress, in recognition of their special place in our society.

2. *Other Reforms*

The achievement of the objectives of the patent system depends in large part on the strength of protection a patent provides. Today a U.S. patent has less than a 50 percent chance of surviving a court challenge. Uncertainty as to the validity and continued reliability of a U.S. patent creates the threat of lengthy and expensive litigation with an uncertain outcome.

a. To improve the presumptive validity of an issued patent, and to reduce the cost and frequency of defending it in court, the President is proposing several significant steps. First, the quality of issued patents will be significantly upgraded by major improvement of the Patent and Trademark Office's filing and classification system. Second, he is urging the Congress again to establish a single court to deal with patent appeals. This court would establish nationwide uniformity in patent law, make litigation results more predictable, and eliminate the expensive and time-consuming forum shopping that characterizes patent litigation. Finally, to minimize the cost and uncertainty of litigation patent validity in the courts, the President will submit legislation to provide for voluntary reexamination of issued patents by the Patent and Trademark Office at the request of any person or the court.

b. One of the world's greatest stores of technical information is in the Patent and Trademark Office files, which include more than four million U.S. Patents. However, the current state of access to the information in these files renders their technical content inaccessible to anyone but patent examiners. The President is asking the Patent and Trademark Office to undertake efforts to provide greater ease of public access and use to these files. These reforms will be undertaken without an increase of public expenditures by adjusting the fee schedule of the patent office so that those who benefit will pay for the services they receive. Legislation supporting these reforms will be submitted to the Congress.

c. The Administrator of the Small Business Administration will establish an Office of Small Business Patent Counsel to assist inventors in the transition from invention to small business by providing the ancillary business that attorneys rarely provide. To encourage the development of technologically-based minority businesses, a similar office will be established in the Office of Minority Business Enterprise and its activities will be coordinated with the SBA. All costs will be met by reprogramming.

Clarifying antitrust policy

Antitrust laws play a specific role in promoting innovation. Vigorous enforcement of antitrust laws spurs competition—and the pressure of competition is a stimulant to the development of innovations that provide a competitive edge. However, antitrust laws are often and mistakenly understood to prevent cooperative activity, even in circumstances where it would foster innovation without harming competition.

The Domestic Policy Review revealed such misunderstanding in industry, universities, and government in instances where cooperative research is permissible, or where cooperation is not permissible.

Industry underinvests in longer-term basic research, largely because the pay-back is difficult to achieve. In long-term research particularly, the President believes some industry cooperation is desirable. This premise led to the cooperative automotive research program, announced by the President and auto industry executives following their meeting at the White House in May 1979.

The President is taking two actions that will clarify antitrust policy and should spur greater research activity by industry:

1. The President is asking the Department of Justice to prepare a guide to clarify its position on collaboration among firms in research and development.
2. The President is requesting the Attorney General, the Chairman of the Federal Trade Commission, and the Secretary of Commerce to initiate

discussions with industry about innovation, antitrust policy formulation, and enforcement. The purpose is to dispel the perception that antitrust policy inhibits innovation and to improve communication between industry, the Justice Department, and the Federal Trade Commission.

Fostering the development of small innovative firms

Small, high-technology firms provide the majority of the new innovations in our economy. The major problems facing entrepreneurs in new firms have been identified as: start-up capital, second-round financing, and early management assistance. The new capital gains structure has loosened the flow of second-round venture capital from private sector sources.

In addition to other actions that generally will benefit smaller R&D firms, the President is taking four specific steps to foster innovation in small, high-technology firms:

1. *National Science Foundation Small Business Innovation Research Program*

The National Science Foundation Small Business Innovation Research Program provides funding to small companies to permit development of a venture analysis for new projects and demonstrate technological feasibility. The program has operated for two years at $2.5 million. It is applauded by both the small and big business communities. It has resulted in projects for which follow-on private-sector funding has been pledged.

The President has decided to expand the NSF program through an increase in FY 1981 of $10 million. In addition, the President is directing the NSF to work with other agencies to determine whether similar programs should be established. The Office of Management and Budget will coordinate development of plans and goals for the expansion of these programs, working toward a goal of approximately $150 million annual funding.

2. *Corporations for Innovation Development*

States or multi-state regions can join in the Federal government's efforts to spur innovation by establishing State or regional "Corporations for Innovation Development" (CID's). The goal is to help alleviate some of the difficulty an entrepreneur confronts in obtaining start-up capital. These CID's would be modeled partly after the successful National Research and Development Corporation in Great Britain and existing state corporations, such as the Connecticut Product Development Corporation. Their functions would include:

- Direct equity funding for the start-up of firms wishing to develop and bring to market a promising, but high-risk, innovation.

- Guidance to potential applicants to the National Science Foundation Small Business Program, including serving as the second-round guarantor in appropriate cases.
- Early management assistance to firms that are funded.
- When otherwise qualified, acting as the recipient of Economic Development Assistance funds for the state or region.

To lead the way for states or regions to establish CID's, the Federal government (through the Department of Commerce) will support two regional CID's in FY 1981. To provide breadth, one of these CID's will be in an industrial region, and the other in a less industrialized State or region. The Federal support will be in the form of loans of $4 million per center, on the condition that the region provide matching funds.

3. *Federal Support for Small R&D Businesses*

Funding for new R&D is a problem for small firms. The small business community correctly believes that given their number, and the significance of their role in the innovation process, they receive a disproportionately low percentage of Federal R&D dollars. To deal with this, the President is directing each agency that contracts for R&D services to:

a. Develop policies ensuring that small businesses are not unfairly excluded from competition for contracts.
b. Publicize, through the SBA and the State or regional CID's, opportunities for bidding that are especially appropriate to small businesses.
c. Report their progress toward increasing small business participation annually to OMB.

4. *General Venture Capital Availability*

As the number of new start-ups increases, the demand for second-round financing will increase. While the capital gains tax changes have increased the flow from taxable private sector investors, the flow will be further encouraged by the following actions the President is taking:

a. The President is directing the Administrator of the Small Business Administration (SBA) to change Part 121.302(a) of the SBA regulations to permit Small Business Investment Companies (SBIC's) and private sector venture capital firms to co-invest in a small firm. The changes are subject to restrictions. There must be an identifiable independent entrepreneur in control of the firm. And there must not be a provision for acquisition by the private sector firm as part of its financing.
b. The Administration already has changed the Employment Retirement Income Security Act (ERISA) regulations to make it permissible for fund managers to invest in small, innovative businesses. In addition, the

President will request the Administrators of ERISA and the SBA to establish an interagency committee to examine what regulatory changes or other means are needed to stimulate investment in small and medium-endowment funds. This will foster further availability of venture capital.

Opening federal procurement to innovations

New technology plays a critical role in promoting innovation. In a free enterprise system, however, marketplace incentives are the crucial motivators. This fact bestows a special responsibility on the Federal government, because it is the Nation's largest single purchaser of goods and services.

In the past, the Department of Defense and the National Aeronautics and Space Administration have shown convincingly the impact that Federal purchasing power can have as a marketplace stimulus. A pilot program at the Department of Commerce—known as the Experimental Technology Incentives Program—has demonstrated that the government can use its purchasing power to spur innovation in areas other than major systems development and high technology. The President will take actions intended to extend this experience to all Federal purchasing.

1. The President is directing the Administrator for Federal Procurement Policy in the Office of Management and Budget to introduce reforms in Federal procurement practices by establishing uniform procurement policies and regulations so as to remove barriers that inhibit the government from realizing benefits of industrial innovation. Special attention is to be given to the most innovative small and minority businesess.

    a. Heads of executive agencies and establishments are being asked to designate senior officials to expedite implementation of new reforms.

    b. Special attention is to be given to substituting performance specifications in place of design specifications, and, wherever feasible, selection will be on the basis of costs over the life of the item, rather than merely the initial purchase price.

2. The President is asking the Administrator, General Services Administration, to expand the New Item Introductory Schedule to publicize, within the Federal government, the existence of new items. To accomplish this, GSA will take steps to inform the business community—particularly small businesses—of the New Item Introductory Schedule and of its benefits.

Improving our regulatory system

Government regulations often influence industrial innovation, stimulating it in some cases and discouraging it in others. For example, some regulations provide incentives for inventing totally new processes to meet regulatory requirements. Other regulations can cause industry decisionmakers to divert resources from exploratory R&D into defensive research aimed only at ensuring compliance with government regulations.

The Carter Administration has a record of being sensitive to the need for a balanced approach to regulations, independently of the Domestic Policy Review on innovation. Previous actions the President already has taken that will have a favorable impact on industrial innovation include:

- Deregulation of airlines and other industries. The President expects the pressure of competition to trigger innovative new ways to cut costs and improve service.
- In environmental, health and safety regulation, the Administration is emphasizing cost-impact analysis to take account of regulatory burdens on industry. The President has formed the Regulatory Analysis Review Group and sent to Congress last spring the Regulatory Reform Act to make regulations more efficient and effective.
- Last month, OMB reported substantial progress in the implementation of Executive Order 12044, which sets goals for improving Federal regulatory practices.
- The President created the Regulatory Council to provide better coordination between the regulatory agencies. The Council is made up of the heads of 35 regulatory agencies. The Council is working to reduce inconsistencies and duplications between regulations, eliminate delays, reduce paperwork and generally keep the cost of compliance down. The Council publishes the *Calendar of Federal Regulations* which contains information about major regulations under development. This is intended to reduce uncertainty about future regulations. All of these reforms show the Administration's continuing efforts to offset negative effects of regulation on societal objectives.

In addition to these actions already taken, the President is announcing today several decisions specifically in connection with improved innovation:

1. The Administrator of EPA will review the agency's programs to determine what further opportunities exist to substitute performance standards for design or specification standards within statutory authority. Specification standards should only be used when they are clearly justified. Regulatory agencies will also be encouraged to explore the possibility of providing dual criteria for either performance and specification standards, thereby allowing individual firms to choose the mode best suited for them.
2. In conjunction with their semiannual regulatory agenda, executive health, safety, and environmental regulatory agencies will prepare five-

year forecasts of their priorities and concerns. Better knowledge of agency plans will allow industry to plan its research and development.

3. The EPA Administrator will develop and publicize a clear implementation policy and set of criteria for the award of "innovation waivers." He will assess the need for further statutory authority.

4. Federal executive agencies responsible for reviewing the safety and efficacy of products will develop and implement a system of priorities. Under these systems, the agencies will identify those products that are most innovative and/or have exceptional social benefits, and expedite their clearance reviews to the extent permitted by applicable statutes. These systems will affect the speed, but not the quality, of the agency's review.

5. To expedite the introduction of new drugs marketed in foreign countries and to expedite the U.S. drug review process, the President is asking the Administrator of the Food and Drug Administration to take steps to assure that our drug clearance process benefits from the foreign experience.

Facilitating labor/management adjustment to technical change

Labor plays an important role in industrial innovation. Perceptions by investors of labor attitudes toward innovation influence the investors' willingness to move ahead. Labor, on the other hand, recognizes the importance of innovation and technological change, realizing that innovations that improve productivity commonly increase the number of workers employed within an industry over the long term. Labor also understands that entirely new industries have been created through innovation. Nevertheless, individual innovations often are perceived as a threat to labor because shifting skill mixes result.

The key to successful adjustment is warning time. Thus, a labor-technology forecasting system, supported cooperatively by labor and management, could be very valuable. Its purpose would be to attempt to forecast technological change within specific industries and to assess the implications for labor of such change. These forecasts and assessments could provide the basis for retraining and other adjustment activities by industry and labor. Labor has been advocating this approach for twenty years. It is long overdue. Therefore:

The President is directing the Secretary of Labor and the Secretary of Commerce to work jointly with labor and management to develop a national Labor/Technology Forecasting System. The President is requesting that they implement this new system in the context of ongoing labor-management activities, in conjunction with agencies responsible for adjustment assistance, and in cooperation with labor/management teams.

Maintaining a supportive climate for innovation

The results of the Domestic Policy Review stressed the importance of a favorable climate in the U.S. receptive to new innovation and of perceived public attitudes toward innovation. Accordingly, the President plans three actions aimed at making a clear public commitment to ensure that innovation in this country thrives in the future.

1. Recognizing that future enhancements in industrial innovation lie primarily in the management/engineering area, the President is asking the Commerce Department and the National Science Foundation to host a National Conference for Deans of Business and Engineering Schools to stimulate improved curriculum development in technology management and entrepreneurship.
2. The President is establishing an award for technological innovation. The existence of this award will provide explicit encouragement to U.S. industry, symbolizing a national commitment to innovation. The awards will consist of a Presidential plaque given to companies in six areas: transportation, communication, health, agriculture and food, natural resources (including energy). The selection criteria will include both technical excellence and commercial impact. The Department of Commerce will be responsible for presenting the President with a list of nominees each year. The awards will be presented annually by the President's Science and Technology Advisor.
3. The President is asking the Productivity Council to form a committee charged with monitoring innovation, developing policies to encourage it, assisting the agencies in implementing these policies, and pursuing the removal of legislative or administrative barriers to the innovation process.

KENDRICK COMMENTARY

The President's initiatives are a good beginning toward a broad and ongoing program for promoting productivity. Keep in mind, however, that industrial innovation is only one aspect of productivity growth—the thirty-three measures initiated under the nine headings are less than one-third of the measures recommended in my paper. Obviously, much more remains to be done. In particular, tax measures designed to eliminate, reduce, or offset the anti-saving/investment biases of the present tax system are the most important levers available—as pointed out by the Joint Economic Committee—to spur innovation and productivity advance more generally. I hope that the administration and Congress will soon begin a thorough reform of the tax system from this point of view—in 1981 if not in 1980. I also hope that expansion of the investment tax credit to cover private R&D would be considered, in addition to a reasonably steady rate of increase in public funding for R&D, in real terms.

The President's initiatives also do not cover a number of other areas of importance to promoting productivity growth: increasing the quality and efficiency of labor, particularly through more and better education and training, and through worker participation in organizational productivity programs; facilitating resource reallocations by increasing the mobility of labor and capital and by adjusting the patterns of natural resource usage; promoting a stronger and steadier rate of economic growth generally through appropriate macroeconomic policies; increasing public investments and current services that would enhance private sector productivity; and increasing efforts by governments at all levels to increase the productivity of governmental operations.

Of potential long-term importance is the President's charge to the Productivity Council to monitor innovation, develop policies to encourage it, assist the agencies in implementing the policies, and pursue the removal of barriers to the innovation process. The charge might well have been broadened to include other aspects of productivity advance. But it seems clear that the staff and other resources available to the Council are insufficient to do an adequate job, even of carrying out the directive as it stands, as discussed in my paper. As recommended there, the resources should be increased.

The establishment of annual Presidential awards for technological innovation is a good idea. But it is curious that the awards are confined to companies in six areas which represent less than half the economy. Later, the number of areas to be recognized should be expanded to include the other major sectors of the economy: construction, manufacturing, trade, finance, and services—private and public (other than health, which is one of the initial sectors).

In conclusion, the President is to be congratulated for making a significant beginning toward reversing the productivity slowdown through his industrial innovation initiatives and some related actions. The important thing is that the initiatives be continued and gradually expanded in scope. It is to be hoped that the National Productivity Council will annually develop proposals for additional measures to accelerate productivity gains and that those which are meritorious will be acted on by the President and the Congress.

University Contributions to The National Energy Program: New Knowledge, New Talent, New Integration

ENERGY ADVISORY COMMITTEE
ASSOCIATION OF AMERICAN UNIVERSITIES
JACK M. HOLLANDER, CHAIRMAN

THE ENERGY PROBLEM FACED BY THE UNITED STATES IS BECOMING WIDELY perceived and increasingly understood. The challenge of the problem is twofold: first, to find the path through the coming period of transition away from dependence on fossil oil and gas that makes available the social and economic benefits of energy yet holds the social and economic costs of the transition to an acceptable level; and, second, to ensure that an appropriate mix of sustainable energy sources will be available when they are needed for the long-term future. To meet this challenge requires both developing and deploying substitute sources and learning how to use less of primary energy to produce an equivalent level of consumer services or amenities, or—more broadly —the same quality of life.

The nation's energy problem arose from a combination of historically decreasing energy prices, which caused high rates of growth in energy consumption and stagnant domestic energy production. In the recent past, U.S. domestic energy supply and demand have been growing increasingly out of balance. Were trends of the recent past to continue (3.4 percent annual growth in energy consumption, 1950–1970), U.S. energy demand would be heading toward a future level of over 200 quads annual primary energy resource consumption by 2010 (up from 76 quads today), whereas U.S. domestic supply would probably be heading toward a future production of less than

100 quads annually in 2010.[1] So great a mismatch would imply future quantities of imports that would probably not be available at any price, and only at very high political and economic costs, if they were available. Therefore, *a primary goal of U.S. energy policy should be to reduce or eliminate the domestic energy supply-demand imbalance so that our dependence on imports can be reduced or even eliminated in the future.* To translate this general goal into specific policies for supply enhancement and/or demand reduction requires that a target be set for a future U.S. supply-demand equilibrium. (Such a target can only constitute a zero-order strategy, because of the inherent uncertainty in estimating future supply and demand, and this uncertainty must be allowed for in setting supply and demand goals.) At what level of energy resource consumption should the targeted U.S. energy supply-demand equilibrium lie? Should it be 150 quads in 2010? 100 quads? Less than 100 quads?

Recent energy demand analyses have indicated that a wide range of supply-demand equilibria are both technically achievable for the United States and consistent with a given level of economic growth. One study has concluded that future energy-consumption levels ranging from about *one-half* to *two times* the present U.S. per-capita energy consumption could be achieved by the year 2010, and that the entire range of these possible futures is consistent with a doubling to tripling of real gross national product (GNP) by 2010, provided that self-consistent policies are followed steadily from now until then.[2] Policies required to achieve the highest energy-growth would need to give priority to government incentives and subsidies to stimulate rapid energy supply increases while keeping prices low to the consumer. Policies to achieve the lowest energy-growth, in contrast,

1. *Energy in Transition, 1985–2010*, Report of the Committee on Nuclear and Alternative Energy Systems (Washington: National Academy of Sciences—National Research Council, 1980).

2. *Alternative Energy Demand Futures to 2010*, Report of the Panel on Energy Demand and Conservation, Committee on Nuclear and Alternative Energy Systems (Washington: National Academy of Sciences, 1979).

Jack M. Hollander is associate director, Lawrence Berkeley Laboratory, University of California.

The opinions and recommendations in this paper are those of the authors and are not intended to represent the official policy or endorsement of the Business–Higher Education Forum or the American Council on Education.

would give priority to measures such as energy-use taxes and mandatory performance standards to stimulate rapid increases in energy efficiency. Not only are these kinds of policies very different in the extremes, but also they represent disparate societies in terms of institutional arrangements and social impacts of energy systems. The actual pathway followed by this country will probably represent a middle course between these extremes that will evolve through deliberate political choices, some of which are now being debated, as well as through future events, both domestic and foreign, which are largely unpredictable.

The role of energy policy is to assist the nation to define and follow a politically and economically efficient trajectory within the wide range of technically achievable possibilities. Economic efficiency requires flexibility of policy and of research such that, as time goes on, signals from consumers' responses to prices, and information flowing in from research and development (R&D) programs, can be fitted together to approach and sustain an effective use of available energy resources. Political efficiency allows the incentives of industry and the processes of government to be meshed so as to facilitate the implementation of these aims. Presently there is considerable uncertainty and disagreement about what such a trajectory would be like. Put simply, we really do not know how much energy this nation will need to use in the future to fulfill its various social goals. The answer will depend partly on technological developments and partly on how the nation ranks its social goals in the future. Nonetheless, policy choices must be made, and are being made, which will greatly influence that future. It is important that these choices be as informed as possible.

THE ROLE OF RESEARCH IN ENERGY POLICY DEVELOPMENT

Serious deficiencies of information impede society and policy makers from setting overall supply-demand goals and developing the components of our future energy system. Some of the needed information can be obtained only through social experience, which has a large element of unpredictability. Other information can be provided by research. An example of the former is public appraisal of technologies. The public viewpoint can be swayed considerably by the information received about random events such as the Three-Mile Island nuclear reactor accident or the Chicago DC-10 airplane crash.

Another example is consumer response to rising energy prices ("price elasticity of demand"): the sign of the effect can be predicted but the magnitude can only be experienced. And the future price of energy itself depends on worldwide political developments that are almost completely unpredictable, although technical factors (e.g., cost of replacement energy) will have a significant influence on the point at which prices stabilize.

On the other hand, research is essential for obtaining many kinds of information and understanding important to energy policy development. A broad spectrum of activities is involved, from "pure" research to research aimed at specific developments.[3] All phases of the research process are equally important to the nation's energy future. Universities have made major contributions to all of them in the past, and we put forward the case in this document that the universities can and must play an increasingly important future role in energy research. It bears emphasis also that whatever our national energy policy may be, an essential element of its evolution and implementation will be the availability of highly trained personnel. The responsibility to provide these personnel falls almost uniquely to the university. Only by maintaining strong instruction and research programs in relevant areas can the university discharge this responsibility.

Consideration of the energy problem lends itself to division into "short" and "long" time periods, because the duration of the coming transition away from dominance of natural oil and gas is expected to be extremely brief in comparison with the long-term future, which will require an energy supply system that is sustainable essentially indefinitely. No sharp demarcation between the short and long terms is implied, and the length of the transition period itself depends on many factors including the growth rate in energy use and the rate of technological progress in developing economically competitive substitute energy technologies. It is important that the transition period

3. We use the following terms to describe the research process: *discipline-oriented basic research* in pure scientific disciplines seeks the discovery and understanding of fundamental phenomena independent of specific energy goals (e.g., plasma physics, geochemistry, surface chemistry). *Goal-oriented basic research* uses the paradigm of basic science but seeks particular kinds of knowledge required in certain energy areas (e.g., research in photovoltaics, combustion, aerosol chemistry, coal-structure chemistry, systems modeling, risk analysis). *Applied research* makes use of existing basic knowledge in the study of particular energy technologies or systems (e.g., research on solar-thermal collectors, chemical engineering studies of coal conversion, reactor safety studies, building energy-efficiency research).

be extended in time, not from a lack of will or sense of urgency about solving the problem, but rather to ensure that the transition is smooth and to provide sufficient time for finding solutions to the multiplicity of problems accompanying the development of long-term sustainable energy systems. An intermediate-term strategy might be followed that allows the nation to ease its dependence on natural oil and gas (e.g., via coal-based synthetic fuels or advanced converter reactors) while not committing to particular long-term systems (e.g., breeder reactors or fusion technologies) for perhaps another half-century. Research has an indispensable role to play in defining the bounds of feasible solutions for both short- and long-term periods.

In the short term, research is needed in the technical and socio-economic sciences to provide an adequate knowledge base for selecting energy policies and for improving the decision-making process itself. *An immediate objective of the nation's short-term energy policy should be to make energy supply goals and energy consumption goals consistent.* A most important question on which this balance depends, and about which there is insufficient knowledge, is the extent to which it is feasible to relieve scarcities in U.S. energy supplies over the next two decades (especially liquid fuels) by technical and institutional measures to increase the efficiency of U.S. energy use and thereby to reduce demand. Research and experience are both needed to answer the following questions:

- At given levels of energy prices, what is the near-term potential for cost-effective energy savings through technical measures to increase end-use efficiency?
- How large are the required investments to bring them about, and how great are the pay-offs, in energy, in money, and in social benefits?
- How long will it take to implement them, and what types of social and economic incentives are needed?
- What should be the balance of government regulatory involvement and financial investment versus private investment to achieve these goals?
- What are the social and economic ramifications of such measures?
- What are the risks and costs of failure?
- Is our institutional and decision-making structure adequate for designing and effecting the needed policies?

On the energy supply side, the corresponding short-term needs for knowledge refer mainly to *the rate at which the domestic energy supply system can be counted on to expand, especially to fill needs for fluid fuels brought about by increased demand and constrained imports.* Setting realistic short-term energy supply targets requires considerably more knowledge than we now have about questions such as:

- What are the constraints to a rapid increase in production and use of domestic coal?
- What are the health and environmental ramifications of a several-fold expansion of U.S. coal use, as called for by some policy scenarios?
- How rapidly can synthetic fuels and shale-oil industries be expected to come on line and reach significant production levels, given today's uncertainties about inflating costs and the environmental impacts of their deployment?
- What is the real situation with respect to domestic and foreign reserves of oil and uranium?
- What will be the costs and near-term producibilities of natural gas from unconventional sources and of oil recovered by tertiary methods?
- How can the costs of coal-based synthetic fuels be reduced to the level of expected oil prices, and when is this crossover likely to occur?
- What are the major issues constraining the expanded use of nuclear power, and how can they best be resolved?
- To what degree can solar heating technologies displace oil and gas use in the next two decades?
- When can solar photovoltaics be expected to reach the stage of economic, as contrasted with technical, feasibility?

Today's research builds the foundation for tomorrow's energy system. *For the long term, the nation needs to develop an energy supply system containing an appropriate mix of technologies that are both sustainable and socially acceptable, and an energy demand structure that is commensurate with the expected future value of energy.* At present we have few, if any, actual long-term supply options; that is, a decision could not be taken and implemented now to deploy any of the known long-term supply technologies in an economically efficient manner with today's technologies. A very considerable amount of research and development is necessary to bring to readiness the nuclear breeder or other advanced reactor options, a wide range of solar-based technologies, use of geothermal energy, and fusion. The nation does not have enough information to make firm choices among these long-term systems now; what is needed is a dedication to a broad and continuous research program that will provide the knowledge base upon which those decisions can be based, as they become necessary.

Today's knowledge is also insufficient to evaluate the comparative risks and impacts of different long-term energy technologies and strategies. Reliable integrated assessments covering the entire spectrum of physical and social risks and impacts need to be done on alternative long-term systems with different mixes of solar, nuclear, coal, and synthetic or shale-derived liquid fuels, and on different long-term strategies including widespread deployment of decentralized and renewable systems. The availability of such assessments could greatly affect policy choices of energy supply alternatives and overall energy strategies. A major issue at present is the comparative costs and risks of renewable (e.g., mostly solar) and conventional energy systems (e.g., nuclear, fossil).

Gaining an understanding of long-term energy demand—the practical and economic limits to the physical efficiency of energy and materials use—is an important and neglected element of the energy problem. Research should be supported that would lead to improving energy-use efficiency in fundamental ways, that would examine the social effects of substitution of one means to supply consumer amenities by others, that would look at the relationship of long-term world energy needs to U.S. supply and demand and to the global situation. We must seriously examine the hard to estimate but possibly overwhelmingly important effects of continuing use of fossil energy technologies on climate and agriculture. Fundamental information is needed about possibilities for geographical rearrangement of man's activities, recycling of materials, enhanced product repair and reuse, and the development of extremely energy-efficient structures and products.

A much better understanding is needed of the societal aspects of alternative energy futures and policies. Government and private decision makers need to become increasingly sensitive to changes in public perceptions of and attitudes toward technology, government, social institutions, and quality of life. A considerably expanded research effort in the social sciences is required to assess these questions and determine their significance for energy policy.

THE ROLE OF UNIVERSITIES IN ENERGY RESEARCH

In the United States, the primary institutions that perform research are industry, the national and other federal laboratories, and the universities. Each has an important role and special capabilities in research, which need to be recognized in designing an overall program of energy research. The potential for cooperative contributions of these research sectors must also be realized.

The main function of industry is to develop technologies and products that meet society's needs and amenities, and to do so at a profit. Industry must not only fulfill existing needs but also anticipate future needs and desires, and develop the required new technologies and products. The growing interest in energy-efficient consumer products, spurred on by both higher energy prices and government energy-performance regulations, has given rise to many new opportunities for industrial production (e.g., energy-efficient automobiles, appliances, and home retrofits). These opportunities are stimulating new programs of industrial applied research dedicated to engineering design, product development, and marketing. Relatively little discipline-oriented basic research is done in industrial laboratories: not only can a company not know whether or when such research will result in practical applications within its sphere of interest, but also it can have little control over the likelihood that the economic benefits of its research will be captured by competitors. Considerably more goal-oriented basic research is done by industry, responding to perceived needs for information related to specific product goals. But for the most part, industry depends on the other research sectors, particularly the universities, to provide the base of scientific and engineering knowledge required as a precursor to the development of new technology. Because of this, it is important that university energy research be sensitive to the needs of industry, upon which our society ultimately depends for the implementation of energy technologies and systems.

The Department of Energy (DOE) national laboratories have a wide and varied role in research. Some of the laboratories are concerned primarily with applied research and development in fields of

143

special interest, and all have become very heavily engaged in energy research. In the conduct of applied energy research, the laboratories have a role complementary to that of industry, and pursue problem areas that would normally be by-passed by industry because the research either has little potential for near-term payback, involves unusually high risk, or involves goals not normally within the usual industrial realm of interest.

Universities and national laboratories have a natural role in research areas that potentially bring large public benefits, hence justify public support, but have private benefits too small to justify participation by individual firms. Most basic research is in this category. Universities and the national laboratories carry out large and varied programs of basic research. Some of the laboratories, with distinguished research traditions going back decades, have become the principal research arms of co-located or participating universities in a number of research areas. This symbiotic university-national laboratory relationship has been extremely productive in the basic physical sciences, and some laboratories are responsible for major national research facilities in certain disciplines such as nuclear and high-energy physics. An increasing amount of goal-oriented basic research in energy problems is being developed by the laboratories. A unique national resource, the national laboratories are administered by universities, for the most part, and should be employed by them to the fullest to enhance the universities' own capabilities in research and training.

The mission of the university has changed dramatically through time. Originally, the university's primary purpose was dissemination of a fixed body of knowledge to students. Today society receives much more from the university, including addition to man's store of knowledge through basic research; integration of the knowledge from many disciplines into the total intellectual structure of society; communication of knowledge and the paradigm of scholarship to the public and, through students, to the next generation of intellectual leadership; and maintenance of the highest intellectual standards of society and leadership in the major fields of human knowledge.

One of the unique facets of the university is the faculty-student relationship, which guarantees a continuing infusion of new talent, not only into the society following completion of the formal education process, but even in a more concentrated and effective way into the intellectual activities of the universities themselves. That intense relationship at universities gives them the ability to respond in a unique way to many of the challenges of the energy problem.

The main vehicle by which the university sustains its intellectual leadership in so many fields is basic research, the process by which scholars pursue their own interests in a quest to enlarge the common understanding of nature, man, and society. In some cases there is no deliberate intent to solve practical problems or achieve specific social ends, whereas in others general or specific goals are in mind. There is strong social justification for public support of both disciplinary and goal-oriented basic research. When answers are needed to pressing practical problems, especially on a short time scale, society draws on the existing body of knowledge. When that stock is inadequate, as in the national effort to conquer cancer or to develop fusion energy as a commercial source of power, any program to develop a practical solution will be hindered until the needed additional knowledge is obtained. To the degree that we know what tomorrow's important needs and problems will be, we can orient today's fundamental research in those directions. (Basic research on materials for photovoltaic conversion is an example of such a case.) To a great extent, however, it is impossible to judge in advance what kind of basic knowledge will prove important to the solution of particular practical problems. Therefore, it is important for society to allow creative minds to be free to follow their own intellectual interests and internal logic, whether or not there are general goals that underlie the support of the research.

Society has received ample returns from its support of discipline-oriented basic research, most of which has been done in universities and university-affiliated laboratories. Countless examples can be cited. The principle of the laser was discovered in the course of disciplinary basic research in atomic physics, and led to a revolution in the field of communications, an entirely new industry, and even a possibly essential link in the development of fusion power. Penicillin was discovered as a byproduct of basic biochemical research; Alexander Fleming was not searching for a cure for bacterial infections. Basic research in nuclear physics and chemistry led to the discovery of fission and transuranic isotopes, which gave rise to an economic source of power for the present and a potential source for millenia. Basic research in biology and chemistry has led to a greatly increased

145

knowledge of the impacts of industrial and other human activities on the environment and human health—knowledge that is essential for the development and implementation of benign future energy technologies.

A significant fraction of university basic research is goal-oriented. In medicine the link between research and application is very strong; rarely does an important discovery in basic biological or medical science not find prompt application to medical diagnosis or treatment. Even though open-heart surgery and organ transplants are products of studies at the frontiers of knowledge of medicine, nonetheless these studies were directed at definite and very practical goals. In the engineering sciences, most university research is directed toward practical application, although a good deal of discipline-oriented basic research is also done; for example, in information theory, computer and systems theory, and the theory of feedback and control systems. In these fields, new knowledge is likely to find ready application, whether or not the research itself is directed to specific goals.

Both discipline- and goal-oriented basic research need to be strong elements of the nation's energy program, devoted to obtaining understanding needed as the basis for energy policy in the short term, as described above, and to creating a foundation of knowledge for development of our long-term energy system. Universities have made strong contributions to both of these areas in the past, and can be expected to do so in the future. However, because of the increasing seriousness and long-term nature of the energy situation and the importance of research on basic and long-term energy problems, greater university involvement is needed. An expanded university role would be in the best interests of both the Department of Energy, which must find and implement solutions, and of the universities themselves, which require participation and involvement in major societal issues in order to maintain their vitality and intellectual leadership.

It is our expectation that the transition to be made by this nation (and the world) from natural oil and gas to synthetic fuels and renewable sources in the coming decades will pose extraordinary demands for people highly trained in the engineering, physical, and social sciences to form the technical and political leadership of our energy future. One of the main functions and responsibilities of the university today is to generate this leadership by attracting talented

146

and inquisitive students to the energy field, and by stimulating and training them through their participation in energy research. This responsibility falls almost uniquely to the university. To fulfill it, universities require substantial and continuous support for energy research, and of the personnel and facilities to conduct that research and the associated instruction.

SUPPORT FOR NEW UNIVERSITY ENERGY RESEARCH

The main point of this paper is to suggest that there are many energy-related research areas (such as those described in the next section) in which increased participation of universities is vitally important to the country's energy future, and to urge a new commitment on the part of government to support this work. It is not our intent to recommend exclusively a single mechanism by which support for new university research should be obtained or managed, although particular mechanisms will be suggested. Nor do we advocate that new energy-related university research be supported at the expense of ongoing federally supported basic research. Although much of the ongoing basic research is not directly energy related, the national interest requires a healthy overall basic science enterprise just as much as it does a strong program of related basic research. These two activities should not be juxtaposed, nor should they be in competition. The total federal R&D budget is adequate to accommodate the nation's basic research needs; what is required is that a small fraction (but larger than today's) of the resources of the large technology R&D structure be devoted to basic research. In the future it is likely that government energy pricing and tax policies will provide considerably augmented revenues to be earmarked for the nation's energy program, and these should provide additional means to support basic energy research needs.

A substantial amount of university research is presently being supported by the Department of Energy ($44 million is received by universities from direct Basic Energy Sciences (BES) funding and via subcontract from national laboratories; this represents about 20 percent of the total BES budget). As we contemplate an expanded university energy-research role, it is important to consider how the interaction between the agency and the universities can be made mutually most beneficial in the future. Our discussion is in the context of present DOE mechanisms for supporting basic research.

Department of Energy support for basic research emanates both from the BES program of the Office of Energy Research (OER) and also to some extent from the mission-directed R&D divisions. We believe that both of these sources should be utilized by the Department to sponsor and manage additional basic research. Both would benefit from such an expansion of scope; the applied research efforts in the R&D divisions would be strengthened by being backed up by fundamental knowledge generated for each program; and the BES programs would become better informed about needs for basic knowledge in a variety of real-world energy problems. There should be close liaison between BES and the technology divisions to ensure the adequacy of design and scope of the total basic research effort.

The Basic Energy Sciences program has for many years managed most of the nation's basic nuclear sciences research, and it has earned a reputation for a productive relationship with the nuclear research community. In these and its other basic science programs, BES has successfully interacted with both the national laboratories and the universities, although to a considerably lesser extent with the latter. Among the reasons for the success of the BES program are the stable funding it has enjoyed over the years, the high level of competence and longevity of service of its staff, a good advisory structure, and perhaps most important of all, recognition by BES that basic research is a particular kind of flower whose health requires appropriate care and sustenance.

The BES program has seen relatively less programmatic change than the rest of the agency during the transformations from the Atomic Energy Commission (AEC) to ERDA to DOE and, as stated, the range of its research activities is narrower than that under discussion here. Support for basic research in DOE has grown over the last three years by an average of about 10 percent annually, in real terms. The operating budget outlay of BES for FY 1980 is $218 million, or about 8.3 percent of the DOE R&D budget.[4] We believe that BES should participate in an expanded goal-oriented basic research program. This would require enlargement of its mission, as well as its budget, to encompass the full range of relevant problems, including those in the social and economic sciences, as described in this docu-

4. This includes R&D in BES, Fossil Energy, Fusion Power, Fission Power, Conservation and Solar Applications, and Environment. Not included are demonstration, defense, or regulatory programs.

148

ment. Also required would be an augmentation of the BES staff in the relevant new disciplines, and a suitably enlarged advisory structure. However, a new administrative unit of DOE would not in principle be required: the BES program exists and functions very well.

A serious difficulty with the present DOE research arrangement is that the class of basic research problems that we term "goal oriented" presently tends to fall into "cracks" between the boundaries of the missions perceived by the basic sciences and the mission-oriented R&D programs. Many researchers have been informed that their proposals are either too basic for the mission-oriented divisions because they do not support short-term goals or milestones, or too applied for the basic science programs because they have particular goal motivations. This problem was in fact recognized by DOE in establishing the Office of Energy Research, but it does not appear to have been solved. We urge that the Department of Energy give considerably greater weight to goal-oriented basic research, both in program management arrangements and in funding allocations.

We believe that the DOE technology divisions should also become a major participant in new basic research. The size of their R&D programs is large and has increased considerably in recent years. The fossil-energy program of the Energy Technology division, for example, grew from $423 million in FY 1977 to $733 million in FY 1979. In spite of these increases, the amount of basic research performed by these divisions is still inadequate, and we believe that each program should be made responsible for a substantial level of goal-oriented basic research relevant to its mission. We encourage the Department of Energy to seek line-item funding for basic research in the programs of each technology division, or for research areas that cut across DOE divisions or programs.

Another approach would be to provide the required funds out of the existing resources of these divisions, by allocating a specified fraction of the budget of each program to basic research within its area of responsibility. We note that the equivalent of 6 percent of the Energy Technology budget would support the entire Basic Energy Sciences program; 1.6 percent, the entire BES chemistry research program. Although we have not studied the matter carefully, we generally concur with the suggestion made by the Office of Science and Technology Policy Working Group on DOE Basic Research (1978 Buchsbaum report) that an agency-wide research coordinating

149

committee would be useful to make recommendations on such allocations as well as for other purposes. Such a committee could facilitate carrying out a policy, which we encourage, of joint support by two or more divisions (e.g., Basic Energy Sciences—Energy Technology or Conservation and Solar—Energy Information Administration) to cover fields of research that are broader in scope than, or overlap, the missions of any one division.

In order for basic research to become successfully integrated into the R&D divisions, not only would new budget allocations be required, but also their missions would have to be redefined to include basic research. Today the R&D program managers interpret their responsibilities in terms mainly of specific short-term product or process goals much like those in industry, which severely inhibits any inclination they might have to support research that cannot easily be justified in terms of short-term goals. There needs to be recognition throughout the agency that applied research and development efforts are usually more successful if they are backed up by basic research, regardless of the time horizons of the program or problem. It is also necessary to buttress the stability of basic research programs undertaken as part of mission-directed R&D, so that they would be less vulnerable to reduction or cancellation in times of fiscal crises. Without such protection, basic research would tend to suffer first as program managers struggle to achieve mission goals in the face of shortages of funds.

In order for DOE to achieve the most productive relationship with universities and affiliated laboratories in a new research effort, it is necessary to decouple short-range government policy goals and corresponding agency responsibilities from the way the agency handles university research. The funding formats currently used by the R&D divisions for research are often not attractive to those doing basic research. Basic research seeks understanding of phenomena, and can only achieve its goal if programs have sufficient continuity to attract and maintain a high level of scholarship. While it is the responsibility of research management to require that researchers demonstrate after a few years that their work can indeed have a direct impact on the problems pursued, high-quality basic research cannot be pursued with use of a management format appropriate for an engineering development program. Thus, fields and projects to be supported, reporting requirements, funding longevity, and other related matters must all be tailored to the sociology of the basic research community if substantial participation of that community is to be achieved. For example, the requirement that researchers respond to requests for proposals (RFPs) to do research with short deadlines and monthly milestone reports is not compatible with the obligation of the university to do scholarly research and to educate students in research. Indeed, with such a mode of interaction it would be difficult for an agency to sustain for long the interest of the basic research community.

It would be beneficial to both the Department and the universities for DOE to establish new ways for interacting with the universities and for responding to unsolicited research proposals from universities (as well as from other institutions such as the national laboratories) for the conduct of discipline-oriented and goal-oriented basic research. The instrument that has been most effective overall in the past for university programs has been the individual or block program grant, and we recommend that this mechanism be employed. The concept of forward funding should be applied to individual grants as well as to institutions, to enhance research continuity. The use of contracts should be limited, as their proscriptive nature can severely constrain investigators in pursuing new ideas that deviate from the original proposal. More emphasis needs to be placed on supporting individuals and organizations of demonstrated productivity and originality, rather than currently popular topics.

There is a critical need for funds for the training and support of high-quality energy research personnel who will be in great demand in future years. In our reference to funds for research, therefore, we include funds for support of top-notch graduate students, postdoctoral fellows, and junior faculty. We urge that the Department of Energy work with the universities to develop a variety of programs to foster graduate education and faculty research in energy-related fields. Specific programs should include support for graduate students, and programs to encourage faculty members to spend sabbatical leaves working in the energy programs of other universities, national laboratories, or in industry. Visiting faculty programs should be designed to make maximum use of the frequently excellent facilities and equipment in industry and the national laboratories. Traineeship programs have also been valuable despite the small size of past programs, and we encourage DOE to reestablish a directed traineeship program as one mechanism to attract top-quality graduate students to the more important energy research fields.

In the social sciences, there is a dearth of experienced people engaged in energy-related research, in contrast with the physical sciences and economics, which have contributed some of their leading researchers to the energy field. Through the support of university social science research in energy, experienced senior faculty could be recruited and young researchers could be encouraged to pursue interests in energy problems.

University participation in major research programs also requires institutional commitments with regard to faculty, students, supporting personnel, equipment, and facilities. The percentage of a research grant to a university that may be devoted to equipment and facilities should be set at a reasonably high level, say 15 percent. Adoption of the practice of providing overhead payments out of funds segregated from direct research funds would also be helpful. Universities will require reasonable assurance of long-term support, and need appropriate provision for long-term financing, if they are to make the necessary commitments to organize and conduct an effective research program.

An approach that could be taken in parallel to or in lieu of utilizing Basic Energy Sciences or the R&D divisions would be to set up a special branch within the Department of Energy to administer university research. One possibility is that the University Affairs and Manpower Office be used for this purpose. This office has primarily a staff function at present, but the control of a significant line item for university research programs could improve the overall direction of DOE research. Were this approach to be followed, care should be exercised to avoid duplication of effort with the existing BES program. The present structure of BES, organized around types of research rather than around client organizations, works well and, if not utilized for new goal-oriented basic research programs, should at least be considered as a model for their management. In any case, the operating management principle should be that the most qualified proposals receive the highest consideration, regardless of their source. Whatever mechanism is chosen, however, it is important that an effective advisory system be implemented for continuously monitoring the overall contributions, quality, and priorities of an augmented basic sciences program. We have not attempted to set out priorities for the research areas suggested in the following section, although we recognize that this is one of the most important tasks in the planning of new research. Not only did time not permit such an evaluation in this exercise, but also we believe that we are not necessarily the right group to do it. A comprehensive review of basic energy research, including an evaluation of the balance among the various areas, could be undertaken by AAU as a follow-on activity if it would be of value to the Department of Energy.

Strong support should be given by the Department to interdisciplinary energy problems and studies. One of the unique aspects of the university is the availability of a broad range of disciplines among its faculty, including many that have not been centrally involved in energy research. Especially needed in the future are contributions from the social sciences. Energy problems are being increasingly recognized as having important political, sociological, economic, and institutional components, whereas most DOE-supported research has been narrowly technical. A growing number of energy research problems also require an integrated approach, demanding participation of several disciplines (e.g., environmental impact studies). The university is the most suitable milieu for such work, not only because of the availability of many disciplines, but also because interdisciplinary education is very important in the training of energy specialists. DOE support could take the form of sponsorship of new interdisciplinary laboratories in technical fields (following the example of the Materials Research Laboratory Program) and support for interdisciplinary graduate study and research groups (e.g., groups such as the Energy Research Laboratory at M.I.T. and the Energy and Resources Group at the Berkeley campus).

The nation badly needs critical socioeconomic research if it is to make progress in many long-term energy issues. Such research can only thrive in a milieu of intellectual independence. Guarantees must be provided for funds to create and maintain an adequate level of scholarly and critically independent intellectual resources, devoted to energy questions, which are required to provide useful social input to energy policy.

In developing this document, we have made the implicit assumption that support for new university energy research will come entirely from the Department of Energy. This may be the case, but it is quite possible that the government will also choose to utilize the

National Science Foundation at least partly for this purpose. In our view this would be entirely appropriate since the universities already have satisfactory working relationships with NSF, and these could be extended readily to cover new program areas developed as part of an expanded university energy research program. We also note with interest that a large program of basic research oriented to development of a very efficient automobile is being organized by the Department of Transportation. Another interesting possibility is a program of joint university/industry research that is being considered by the National Science Foundation.

Whatever mechanisms are instituted for funding new university research, they should be designed in such a way as to strengthen the interactions among universities, industry, and the national laboratories. It would be useful for the government to consider fiscal or other mechanisms that would encourage industry to support university research. Such a university-industry interaction would sharpen faculty awareness of the industrial environment and would assist university researchers in orienting basic research objectives toward the most relevant energy goals.

A major requirement for an enhanced program of energy research in this country is better communication, coordination, and cooperation among the members of that unique American "research triangle": the universities, the federal laboratories, and industry. Each has skills, attributes, and facilities that are complementary to those of the others, and each can make contributions to the work of the others. Today the interaction among them is inadequate. The universities should, as part of their initiative for expanded basic energy research, work closely with the Department of Energy to delineate and develop new relationships and interactions among the three research sectors. The Department, on its part, should encourage and support cooperative basic research programs and high-level research coordination among these sectors. This symbiosis will substantially increase the effectiveness and efficiency of the entire national energy research effort.

A continuous liaison is also needed between the universities and the research planners of the Department of Energy. This liaison could be with the DOE Energy Research Advisory Board (ERAB), or with the research coordinating committee proposed by the OSTP panel. A small liaison staff could transmit information in both directions, channeling university input to the Department and providing information to university presidents and deans about the methods of interactions and funding that are working most (and least) effectively. It would be appropriate to place responsibility for the liaison staff with the Association of American Universities (AAU).

RESEARCH NEEDS

This section contains brief descriptions of energy topics in which further basic research is needed. This review is neither exhaustive nor uniform in coverage, but it does focus on a selection of important problems that should be of interest to the Department of Energy. The following does not provide descriptions of or commentary on the extensive and diverse programs of basic energy and nonenergy research presently supported by the federal government. These are new energy research needs, which call upon the full spectrum of individual and institutional capabilities, and include both discipline- and goal-oriented basic research. Even though this discussion is not complete, we include it in order to support our recommendation of an expanded university energy-research role by specific documentation of the tremendous range of basic problems that not only need to be solved but also can provide challenging research and instructional opportunities for university faculties and students for many years to come.

We believe that all of the research areas described here are suitable, and important, for Department of Energy support, in coordination with other federal agencies that have responsibilities in some of the areas. We urge that the Department increase the scope of its program to encompass them.

Energy demand and end-use

The expected increasing price of energy in the coming decades will in principle provide many economic opportunities for increasing the efficiency of energy use. Great uncertainty exists throughout the economy, however, in the *levels* of efficiency that are technically achievable at given energy prices. It is extremely important that these uncertainties be reduced by research, so that short-term energy supply production targets can be set at realistic levels, and better assessments made of our probable long-term energy requirements.

In the buildings sector, better understanding is needed of the factors contributing to energy use, including design components

155

(e.g., windows, envelope, insulation) and construction factors (e.g., air infiltration). The principles of energy- and optically-efficient lighting are poorly known. Improved theoretical methods for modeling energy use in buildings are required as a prerequisite to the design of enforcable building performance standards. The buildings sector uses 36 percent of U.S. primary energy, and the potential savings from increased efficiency are very great, probably over 50 percent (of current building energy use) in three decades.

Basic research in the transportation sector is needed to obtain knowledge required for development of extremely energy-efficient engines, vehicles, and transportation systems. Included should be fundamental properties of fluids that might be used in advanced engine cycles. Basic research in many aspects of the chemistry of combustion could lead to design of more efficient and less polluting engines, especially in the case of diesel engines. Engine efficiency can also be markedly improved by the design of "smart" control systems that use advanced microelectronics. Vehicle efficiency can be increased by studies of air drag at operating speeds.

In industry, research is needed in a number of areas, some of them of major scope. Optimal changes to improve industrial productivity are often multipurpose, so certain areas not specifically focused on energy may well have the greatest impact on energy. Many long-existing areas of study have been relatively neglected in modern research. For example, fundamental research on basic materials processing (such as paper and steel) and exploration of new basic materials processes are needed. Basic mechanical studies should be carried out on friction and lubrication, control of fluid flow, and (at the microscopic level) fundamentals of separation of materials by processes such as osmosis or adsorption. Heat transfer should be more deeply examined, e.g., at surfaces, in boiling, and in two-phase flow. Studies of sensors are needed to facilitate application of automatic control systems.

The present U.S. energy system is far from optimized in regard to matching of the type, thermodynamic quality, and unit scale of energy supply with end-use function. For example, about one-third of U.S. electricity supply is used for heating and cooling, functions that do not require energy of such high thermodynamic quality. Both economic and energy efficiency would suggest that energy should be supplied only in the quality needed for the task at hand. Competing goals, such as convenience, often work in the opposite direction (e.g., use of electricity for residential heat) and these should be considered in any analysis. Obtaining correlations and analyses of the energy end-use spectrum, according to these characteristics, is an important research need.

Basic thermodynamic theory is a subject that is central to gaining an understanding of how well real processes can perform when they operate at real, non-zero rates. Thermodynamics research can clarify how closely maximum efficiencies can be approached, and has a great bearing on the future design of engines.

A wide variety of research challenges in the social and economic sciences complement those in the physical and engineering sciences. In economics, a fuller understanding is needed of fundamental relationships between energy consumption and economic activity. Basic studies in energy/economy modeling are required, and in this connection studies should be pursued of fundamentally important economic parameters such as the long-term price elasticity, substitutabilities of energy demand, and the impacts of energy supplies and prices on productivity.

Engineering and economic analyses of energy use, and policy formulation, are hindered today by a serious lack of data. Accurate, highly disaggregated and up-to-date energy data bases should be developed expeditiously. These should include time-series and cross-sectional studies on U.S. and foreign energy consumption, dating well before 1973.

Social, institutional, and political barriers impede economically efficient investments in increasing energy efficiency. Social science research is needed to provide an understanding of these barriers, so that effective policy tools can be designed to overcome them. Economics, sociological and political science research are needed to gain a better understanding of consumer decision making about durable goods, such as refrigerators, air-conditioning, automobiles and campers, and about market and non-market factors that influence these decisions.

Policy studies are needed to increase understanding of the types of government actions that are appropriate, effective, and efficient in fostering energy conservation goals and in influencing specific energy supply and end-use technologies, systems, and practices. Attention needs to be placed on the role of tax and pricing policy, information, regulatory practices, equity and distributional impacts of alternative policies and actions, and impacts of delays in decision making.

Energy supply technologies

1. *Fossil fuels*. The increasing costs of conventional fuels will make possible the commercial development of substitute and non-conventional fossil technologies that were considered uneconomic only a few years ago. Because the economics have been so uncertain, the base of knowledge required for establishing viable, large-scale industries has been slow to develop and is still quite inadequate. Basic research is essential in a number of areas related to fossil fuel supplies.

Economic production of synthetic fluid fuels from coal requires considerable basic chemistry and chemical engineering research. The presently available coal-conversion technologies are old, inefficient, and expensive. To arrive at new ideas and new processes it is necessary to have a better understanding of the chemical nature of coal and of the mechanisms of coal gasification, liquefaction, and fuel synthesis from CO and hydrogen. The performance of catalysts in these processes is not entirely satisfactory, and basic studies are needed to produce better and cheaper catalysts.

Oil from shales is an extensive potential substitute fossil source, but today's understanding of the shales is very inadequate, and basic research is needed on the chemical, physical, and mechanical properties of these materials and their derivatives. The environmental problems surrounding shale development may be severe, and serious environmental research should be undertaken so that possible impacts can be evaluated before production is initiated.

To increase the efficiency of oil production, tertiary recovery techniques are being investigated. This is an extremely complex chemical engineering problem, and much remains to be learned in spite of continuing extensive industry research. Major basic research challenges exist in the areas of surface physics and chemistry of multicomponent systems in solid porous media.

As the supplies of low-cost natural gas become depleted, attention is being paid to the potential for increased supplies from unconventional sources of gas from low-permeability media. Basic geological and geochemical understanding of these media are needed if practical ways are to be devised to increase the permeability. Basic physical studies are also needed to confirm predicted locations of tight sources. Associated materials problems are severe, and require fundamental study.

Research is also needed on the social and institutional determinants of resource exploration and development as a basis for choosing and evaluating government tax and land-use policies, and understanding market structure issues.

2. *Solar energy technologies.* The production of synthetic fuels from solar energy may be the most important long-term application of solar energy. The basic chemistry of photochemical conversion has yet to be worked out, and many years of fundamental studies are necessary before engineered systems can be designed. Thermochemical, electrochemical, and biochemical conversion schemes also need basic investigation. For example, techniques of genetic engineering might lead to micro-organisms that would permit fermentation at higher temperatures and in higher alcohol concentrations, both of which could have major consequences for biomass conversion; the longer-range goal would be micro-organisms that could directly produce long-chain hydrocarbons in fermentation processes. This is a top-priority field of basic research.

There is need for basic biological solar energy research in the related disciplines of genetics and microbiology, biochemistry, and biochemical engineering devoted to the objective of producing fuels and chemical feedstocks efficiently from solar energy processes. The growth of plants for food and fuel is currently an energy intensive activity. Can new plants be found that fix their own nitrogen, that fix carbon at lower light and CO_2 levels? What controls these processes, and how can they be manipulated to man's energy benefit?

3. *Materials sciences research.* Materials problems are of central importance in almost all energy technologies. Materials that would permit conventional fossil or nuclear-fueled boilers to operate at even slightly higher temperatures—hence efficiencies—could have dramatic economic consequences; inner wall materials problems may be among the most serious to be encountered in progress toward fusion power; and materials problems are central in the development of solar energy technologies. Costs and reliability are among the major issues. There are many areas for important basic research in metals, ceramics, corrosion, high-temperature performance and in thin films of particular importance in solar work. Basic solid-state research,

including studies of both crystalline and amorphous semiconductors, is very important for possible energy conversion systems.

4. *Nuclear fission.* Research on the entire nuclear fuel cycle is needed. The technological, safety, security, economic, and social implications of alternative fuel cycles must be developed, with special attention to problems of nuclear weapons proliferation, waste disposal, and public safety. Substantial reactor research is needed even for current light water reactor designs. Some of the important cross sections for burning of transuranic species are still only crudely known. Much more research is needed on advanced converter and breeder reactor systems.

5. *Nuclear fusion.* The U.S. fusion R&D program has proceeded nearly to the point of demonstrating the scientific feasibility of nuclear fusion. Subsequent to that demonstration, the technology will have to be developed for engineering achievability, acceptable environmental characteristics, and reasonable cost. It is yet too early to commit to a single technological approach, and premature commitment could be very costly. It is very important that exploration of alternative paths to fusion be supported, as the investment in diversity of approaches is minimal compared with the potential payoff of developing the most attractive form of this technology on a timely schedule. A vigorous basic research program should be pursued, on fundamental fusion science, on alternative plasma confinement configurations and heating techniques, on materials and design problems related to the techology of fusion reactors, on analysis of environmental characteristics, and on engineering and economic practicality.

6. *Basic geology and geochemistry.* Development of a practicable nuclear waste isolation system requires improved fundamental knowledge of rock properties and chemical behavior of actinide-element species in a variety of rock-water systems. Basic geochemical research is required for geothermal energy development, including development of geophysical methods for geothermal reservoir identification and assessment, studies of chemical equilibria in high-temperature brine media, and assessments of environmental impacts of geothermal systems. Experimental and theoretical modeling studies are needed to determine the feasibility of use of aquifers for thermal energy storage.

7. *Energy storage, conversion, and transmission.* Basic electrochemical and thermochemical studies are required to build a founda-

tion for development of improved batteries and other electrochemical systems. The possible wide application of hydrogen as a carrier and secondary source of energy in the future requires solution of many fundamental chemical problems relating to its storage, transmission, and use. There is also need for research related to conversion to electrical energy by magnetohydrodynamic and thermionic methods. Detailed fundamental studies of materials and superconducting systems are required.

Research should aim at developing conversion processes that best match future fuel supplies, for example, the substitution of electrochemical or photochemical processes for current thermal chemical processes, so that more appropriate use can be made of electricity and solar energy than only as heat sources.

Progress in the technology and economics of long-distance transmission of electric power may alleviate the problem of power plant siting by increasing the distance between plant and consumer, and possibly by co-locating several plants to concentrate the safety problem, and introducing economies of fuel handling or reprocessing.

Impacts of energy systems

Basic research in the environmental and life sciences has suffered from probably the greatest degree of instability of any government supported energy-related research. The problem has been at least in part jurisdictional, as exemplified by the uncertain and shifting responsibilities for environmental studies between AEC, then ERDA and DOE, and the Environmental Protection Agency. EPA has generally seen its responsibility as mainly regulatory, and has not supported a sufficiently strong program of basic research.

Research on the environmental, health, and social impacts of energy technologies is an extremely important component of the overall knowledge base required for their development and implementation. Lack of needed knowledge of impacts increases the time required for technology implementation and, especially in the case of large-scale systems, adds to their costs far in excess of the costs of obtaining the knowledge.

The Department of Energy should bear a major responsibility for basic research on the environmental, health, and social impacts of the energy technologies and systems for which it has development responsibility. A number of different types of research are involved, from the most integrated and generic to specific impacts of individual technologies. The Office of Energy Research should be assigned a major responsibility for the former, to be worked out with the Assistant Secretary for Environment, and the technology R&D programs should carry major responsibility for specific impact studies.

Several particularly important areas for DOE research are highlighted in the following. Basic chemistry research is needed to gain an understanding of the chemical formation of pollutants from (primary) stationary and mobile sources, and of pollutant transformations and transport in the atmosphere and in terrestrial and aquatic ecosystems. The national program for accelerated production of shale oil and coal-derived synthetic fuels increases the urgency to understand the nature of the new chemical species that may be introduced into our air and water. Basic engineering studies, derived from the above, are required as a prerequisite for the design of improved environmental control strategies.

A wide variety of fundamental biological and medical research efforts are needed to understand the impacts of energy-related pollutants on man's health and on ecological systems. Today's understanding is insufficient and leaves great uncertainty about the adequacy (or over-conservatism) of present environmental standards and about the requirements and directions for future standards. Quantification of the effects of pollutants should be sought by retrospective epidemiological studies on large populations, where possible. Such research, using records from major metropolitan areas for periods before and after reduction of certain pollutants, could provide important data on the consequences of long-term human exposure to the products of fossil-fuel combustion. Long-term impacts of fossil-fuel combustion on climate are an extremely important aspect of this problem.

Research is needed to assess the impacts of energy conservation measures, for example, the risks to health brought about by use of more insulation and tightening of building envelopes to reduce air infiltration. Such risks could arise from emanations of chemical compounds and radiation from building materials, as well as from indoor activities such as gas cooking and heating. Basic research is needed on mechanisms of and ways to inhibit pollutant release, as well as materials studies underlying the development of energy-efficient and environmentally clean ventilation systems.

Further basic studies on risk assessment are essential. Better methods are needed for the quantitative estimation of risks to human health and safety from energy technologies, including nuclear reactors, fossil-fuel systems, dams, and renewable solar-derived systems. Understanding is also needed of the widely divergent public attitudes toward different energy technologies and non-energy risks such as automobiles and earthquakes. Knowledge of the characteristics that distinguish acceptable from unacceptable social risk will assist society to decide "how safe is safe enough?"

Environmental economics is an increasingly important field. The impacts of energy sources and energy use on the environment have been limited to some extent by a maze of regulations, but at great cost to energy producers and consumers in money, resources, and time. One of the greatest challenges to economists and policy analysts is the reconciliation of the nation's energy and environmental goals, i.e., by development of more cost-effective techniques for preserving and enhancing environmental quality.

Basic socioeconomic issues

Socioeconomic perspectives have been the weakest link in U.S. energy policy, not in small part because of the almost complete lack of research in these fields. The Department should include this research area in its programs, especially in the basic energy sciences. Important obstacles to the implementation of energy supply systems or energy conservation will increasingly be recognized to contain significant political, sociological, economic, institutional, and environmental components. The intellectual and disciplinary breadth of the university is extremely important for providing the insights required.

Much less is known about the social impacts of energy systems than about their physical impacts. Sociopolitical assessments are needed of alternative energy sources at the regional level, renewable vs. conventional energy systems, and centralized vs. decentralized technologies. The socioenvironmental impacts of synthetic fuels and solar energy technologies are much less well understood than those of coal and nuclear systems.

Identification and understanding are required of the interactions among individuals and groups over time as they shape political, social, and economic forces. Specific basic questions include penetration and acceptance of new technologies, incorporation of social costs into public decision making, and potential impacts on energy use of evolutionary social trends (e.g., voluntary or "noneconomic" energy conservation) and individual behavioral changes. Energy policy makers also need to understand better organizational and community behavior toward choices of energy alternatives, including government units, community groups, utilities, interest groups, and industrial firms. Values, risks, environmental factors, and bureaucratic behavior all need to be considered by sociological and economic research. A broader and deeper understanding of how energy markets work is imperative.

The economic assessment of alternative future energy technology mixes can be helped substantially by the further development and application of energy modeling of the type demonstrated in a recent National Academy of Sciences study.[5] Engineering estimates of the costs, efficiencies, and environmental impacts of candidate energy technologies are fitted together in a manner permitting concurrent estimation of promising technology mixes along with prices for the primary, intermediate, and end-use forms of energy that can sustain these mixes. Uncertainty about the parameters of cost, efficiency, productivity, and consumer behavior is recognized by sensitivity analyses in which these parameters are varied, and by models in which these uncertainties are treated as diminishing over time as research is set in motion, at a cost, to that end.

SUMMARY AND CONCLUSIONS

The energy problem

The challenge of our nation's energy problem is twofold: first, to find the path through the coming period of transition away from dependence on conventional oil and gas that makes available the social and economic benefits of energy yet holds the social and economic costs of the transition to an acceptable level; and, second, to ensure that an appropriate mix of sustainable energy sources will be available when they are needed for the long-term future. *To meet this challenge requires both developing and deploying substitute sources and learning how to use less of primary energy to produce an equiv-*

5. "Energy Modeling for an Uncertain Future," Supporting Paper 2, Committee on Nuclear and Alternative Energy Systems Study, National Academy of Sciences, Washington, D.C., 1978.

alent level of consumer services or amenities, or—more broadly— the same quality of life.

Recent energy demand analyses have indicated that a wide range of supply-demand equilibria are both technically achievable for the United States in the future and consistent with a given level of economic growth. The role of energy policy is to assist the nation to define and follow a politically and economically efficient trajectory within the wide range of technically achievable possibilities. Presently there is considerable uncertainty and disagreement about what such a trajectory would be like. Put simply, we really do not know how much energy this nation will need to use in the future to fulfill its various social goals. The answer will depend partly on technological developments and partly on how the nation ranks its social goals in the future. Nonetheless, policy choices must be made, and are being made, which will greatly influence that future. An important function of research is to make these choices as informed as possible.

Energy research needs

In the short term, research is needed in the technical and socioeconomic sciences to provide an adequate knowledge base for selecting energy policies and for improving the decision-making process itself. An immediate objective of energy policy should be to make the nation's energy supply goals and energy consumption goals consistent. At present, on the demand side, we have insufficient knowledge of the extent to which it is feasible to relieve scarcities in U.S. energy supplies over the next two decades (especially liquid fuels) by technical and institutional measures to increase the efficiency of U.S. energy use and thereby to reduce demand. Again, these questions should be answered:

- At given levels of energy prices, what is the near-term potential for cost-effective energy savings through technical measures to increase end-use efficiency?
- How large are the investments required to bring about these energy savings, and how great are the pay-offs, in energy, money, and in social benefits?
- How long will it take to implement them, and what types of social and economic incentives are needed?
- What should be the balance of government regulatory involve-

165

ment and financial investment versus private investment to achieve these goals?

- What are the social and economic ramifications of such measures?
- What are the risks and costs of failure?
- Is our institutional and decision-making structure adequate for designing and effecting the needed policies?

On the supply side, the corresponding short-term knowledge gaps refer mainly to the rate at which the domestic energy supply system can be counted on to expand. Setting realistic short-term energy supply targets requires research to answer these questions:

- What are the constraints to a rapid increase in production and use of domestic coal?
- What are the health and environmental ramifications of a several-fold expansion of U.S. coal use, as called for by some policy scenarios?
- How rapidly can synthetic fuels and shale-oil industries be expected to come on line and reach significant production levels, given today's uncertainties about inflating costs and the environmental impacts of their deployment?
- What is the real situation with respect to domestic and foreign reserves of oil and uranium?
- What will be the costs and near-term producibilities of natural gas from unconventional sources, and of oil recovered by advanced methods?
- How can the costs of coal-based synthetic fuels be reduced to the level of expected oil prices, and when is this crossover likely to occur?
- What are the major issues constraining the expanded use of nuclear power, and how can they best be resolved?
- To what degree can solar heating technologies displace oil and gas use in the next two decades?
- When can solar photovoltaics be expected to reach the stage of economic, as contrasted with technical, feasibility?

For the long term, a very large knowledge base is required for development of an energy supply system containing an appropriate mix of technologies that are both sustainable and socially acceptable, and an energy demand structure that is commensurate with the expected future value of energy. A broad and continuous research program employing many disciplines is necessary to answer the following questions:

- What should be the relative contributions of nuclear and solar technologies in our long-term energy supply system?
- How soon can nuclear fusion be expected to become an economically viable and competitive energy source?
- What are the relative physical and social risks and impacts of alternative long-term energy systems and strategies?
- What are the practical and economic limits to the physical efficiency of energy and materials use over the long run?
- What are the ramifications of fundamental changes in social goals, social institutions, and perceptions of quality of life?

DOE support of basic energy research

Each of the questions cited above represents but a small part of the vast body of knowledge that is required for the nation to chart its course smoothly through the transition period and develop a long-term energy system by the time it is needed. In totality, the challenges to research are probably without precedent, over the entire research spectrum from the most basic to the most applied. An especially important component of energy research is that which is motivated by particular energy goals but is "basic" in every other sense. We focus on goal-oriented basic research for two reasons: first, it appears to have the weakest institutional base within the Department of Energy (DOE), and, second, the universities are capable of making a much larger contribution in this area than they are doing at present.

We urge that the *Department of Energy give considerably more support to goal-oriented basic research.* A difficulty with the present DOE research arrangement is that goal-oriented basic research tends to fall into "cracks" between the boundaries of the missions perceived by program managers in the basic sciences and the mission-directed research and development (R&D) programs. Many researchers have been informed that their proposals are either too basic for the mission-directed divisions because they do not support short-term goals or milestones, or too applied for the basic science programs because they have particular goal motivations. This problem was in fact recognized by DOE in establishing the Office of Energy Research (OER), but it does not appear to have been solved. We urge that renewed atten-

167

tion be given by the Department to goal-oriented basic research, both in program management arrangements and in funding allocations.

Both the mission-directed R&D divisions and the OER basic energy sciences programs should support more goal-oriented basic research. This increase in level and scope would work to the benefit of both; the applied R&D efforts would be strengthened by being backed up by fundamental knowledge in each program; and, the basic research programs would become better informed about real needs for basic research in a variety of energy areas.

We encourage the agency to seek line item funding for basic research in the program of each technology division, or for research areas that cut across DOE divisions or programs. Another approach would be to allocate appropriate amounts from the existing resources of the R&D divisions. A mechanism would have to be established to determine what level is "appropriate" for each program. (The basic research "tax" would not normally need to be large; as an example, 8 percent of the budget of the fossil energy program in the Energy Technology division equals the entire budget for chemical sciences research in the OER Basic Energy Sciences [BES] program.) Although we have not carefully studied the matter, we generally concur with the suggestion made by the Office of Science and Technology Policy (OSTP) Working Group on DOE Basic Research (1978 Buchsbaum report) that an agencywide research coordinating committee would be useful for recommending the levels of such allocations, as well as for other purposes. Such a committee could facilitate carrying out a policy, which we encourage, of joint support by two or more divisions (e.g., Basic Energy Sciences/Energy Technology, or Conservation and Solar/Energy Information) to cover fields of research that are broader in scope than, or overlap, the missions of any one division.

It is necessary to redefine, or at least clarify, the missions of the R&D divisions so that they include basic research relevant to particular missions. Today these missions heavily emphasize specific short-term product or process goals much like those in industry, which severely inhibit the support of basic and long-term research that cannot be easily justified in terms of short-term goals. People with experience in basic research must be added to the staffs of the R&D divisions to manage basic research programs. Stability of basic research programs undertaken as part of mission R&D is especially important so that they will be less vulnerable to reduction or cancellation in times of fiscal crises. Without such protection, basic research would tend to suffer first as program managers struggle to achieve mission goals in the face of shortages of funds.

The funding formats used by the R&D divisions need to be made more attractive to those doing basic research. *Selection of fields and projects to be supported, reporting requirements, funding longevity and other related matters must all be tailored to the sociology of the basic research community if substantial participation of that community is to be achieved.* The goals of basic research can only be attained if programs have sufficient continuity to attract and maintain a high level of scholarship. While it is the responsibility of research management to require that researchers demonstrate after a few years that their work can indeed have a direct impact on the problems pursued, basic research cannot properly be administered with use of management formats appropriate for engineering development. The requirement that researchers respond to requests for proposals (RFPs) to do research with short deadlines and monthly milestone reports is not compatible with scholarly research or the education of students in research.

The Basic Energy Sciences (BES) program of OER has been notably successful in managing discipline-oriented basic research, and may be appropriate for the management of new programs of goal-oriented basic research. We believe that *the BES budget should be increased and the scope of its mission enlarged to encompass the full range of relevant problems, including those in the biological, engineering, environmental, physical, and socioeconomic sciences.* We note that an amount equal to 6 percent of the Energy Technology budget would allow for a doubling of the present BES program.

Expanded university participation in energy

Universities have an almost unique ability and responsibility to contribute to the nation's energy future, by conducting basic research, by training personnel, and by integrating knowledge across disciplines. Universities have made strong contributions to basic energy research in the past. Because of the increasing seriousness and long-term nature of the energy situation and the importance of creating a more substantial base of knowledge for both the short and long terms, greater university involvement is needed. *An expanded university role would be in the best interests of both the Department of Energy,* which must find and implement solutions, *and the universities themselves,* which require participation and involvement in major societal issues in order to maintain their vitality and intellectual leadership.

Scientific and engineering expertise at universities can assuredly make major contributions in problem areas related to energy supply systems. Equally important is their potential contribution to increasing the efficiency of the U.S. energy system. Especially significant university contributions can be expected in areas needing open and unfettered exploration of new concepts and controversial issues. In the study of socioeconomic problems, which are subject to wide differences of view, it is critical that the agency support the kind of scholarly and critically independent intellectual resources that are needed to provide useful social input to energy policy.

At the very heart of university research is the faculty-student relationship, which guarantees a continuing infusion of new talent, not only into the society following completion of the formal education process, but even in a more concentrated and effective way into the intellectual activities of the universities themselves. That intense relationship at universities gives them the ability to respond in a unique way to many of the challenges of the energy problem. The transition to be made by this nation (and the world) from natural oil and gas to synthetic and renewable energy sources in the coming decades will pose extraordinary demands for people highly trained in the engineering, physical, social, and economic sciences to form the technical and political leadership of our energy future. One of the main functions and responsibilities of the university is to generate this leadership by attracting talented and inquisitive students to the energy field, and by stimulating and training them through their participation in energy research.

The Department of Energy should develop programs to foster graduate education and faculty research in energy-related fields. Specific programs should include support for graduate students, and programs to encourage faculty members to spend sabbatical leaves working in the energy programs of other universities, national laboratories, or in industry. The frequently excellent facilities and equipment of industry and the national laboratories should be used to maximum advantage in these programs. Support should also be provided for post-doctoral and junior faculty. Traineeship programs are another mechanism that should be used to attract top-quality graduate students to important energy research fields.

University participation in major research programs requires institutional commitments regarding faculty, students, supporting personnel, facilities, and capital equipment. The percentage of a research grant to a university that may be devoted to equipment and facilities should be set at a reasonably high level. Funds need to be available to provide the sophisticated capital equipment required for front-line research. Adoption of the practice of providing overhead payments out of funds segregated from direct research funds would also be helpful. Universities require reasonable assurance of long-term support, and need appropriate provision for long-term financing, if they are to make the necessary commitments to organize and carry out an effective research program.

The Department of Energy should look to leadership in energy research wherever it is found. It is important that DOE funds be focused for maximum effectiveness, and not be spread too thinly. Universities should be allowed, and encouraged, to compete on an equal footing with federally supported institutions for funding from an augmented DOE basic research program. The national laboratories and industry have special skills, attributes, and facilities that are complementary to those of the universities. Indeed, each member of this unique American "research triangle" can make important contributions to the work of the others, and an enhanced symbiotic relationship among them will substantially increase the effectiveness and efficiency of the entire national energy research effort. To this end, *the Department should encourage and support cooperative basic research programs and high-level research coordination among universities, federal laboratories, and industry.*

We recommend that the Department give strong support to interdisciplinary energy programs and studies. One of the unique aspects of the university is the availability of a broad range of disciplines among its faculty, including many that have not been centrally involved in energy research. Energy problems are being increasingly recognized as having important political, sociological, economic, and institutional components, whereas most DOE-supported research has been narrowly technical. A growing number of energy research problems also requires an integrated approach, demanding participation of several disciplines (e.g., environmental impact studies). The university is the most suitable milieu for such work, not only because of the availability of many disciplines, but also because interdisciplinary education is very important in the training of energy specialists. DOE support could take the form of sponsorship of new interdisciplinary technical laboratories (following the example of the Materials Research Laboratory Program) and support for interdisciplinary graduate study and research groups (e.g., groups such as the Energy Research Laboratory at M.I.T and the Energy and Resources Group at the Berkeley campus).

A continuous liaison is needed between the universities and the research planners of the Department of Energy. Responsibility for the university side of this liaison would be appropriate for the Association of American Universities.

RECOMMENDATIONS

The Energy Advisory Commitee's recommendations are summarized as follows:

- The Department of Energy should give considerably greater support to basic research oriented to the goal of building the knowledge base about energy production and use that our nation requires if it is to bring about a smooth and economically efficient transition from historical dependence on cheap fossil fuels to a long-term, energy-efficient system.
- Universities have an almost unique ability and responsibility to contribute to the nation's energy future: by conducting basic research, by providing talent and trained personnel, and by integrating knowledge across disciplines. The Department of Energy should remove barriers that presently constrain the universities from making their full contributions in all these areas.
- Programmatic gaps between DOE divisions that inhibit the conduct of important energy research should be eliminated. At present, much goal-oriented basic research tends to be considered too basic by the DOE mission-oriented R&D programs, and too applied by the DOE-OER basic sciences programs. Flexibility of research goal definition and funding formats, receptivity to unanticipated new directions, and guarantees of intellectual independence must be included in an enlarged DOE basic research program.
- A significant fraction of the budgets of the DOE mission-directed

R&D divisions should be allocated for goal-oriented basic research. If the programs are managed by those divisions, the program staffs must be augmented to include experts in the relevant basic research areas.

- The budget of the DOE-OER basic energy sciences program should be increased and the scope of the program enlarged to include goal-oriented basic research in areas beyond the presently included disciplines, in the biological, engineering, environmental, physical, and socioeconomic sciences.

- Specific mechanisms appropriate to guide and administer an enlarged DOE basic research program should be worked out by the agency. In general we endorse the suggestions made by the OSTP Working Group on DOE Basic Research (1978 Buchsbaum report). We especially favor the idea of an agencywide basic research coordinating committee, with advisory subgroups in appropriate goal-oriented and disciplinary areas, and with representation of universities, federal laboratories, and industry. Joint support of research cutting across DOE divisions, with line-item funding, is encouraged.

- The Department of Energy should give renewed emphasis to fostering a management climate in which university research can thrive—one that is tailored to both the sociology and the breadth of the basic research community. Fundamental requirements for a high-quality basic research program include continuity sufficient to attract and maintain the highest level of scholarship, and adequate support for equipment and facilities. Continuing liaison is needed between the universities and the Department's research planners, for example, between DOE's ERAB (Energy Research Advisory Board) and AAU (Association of American Universities).

- The Department should develop programs to foster graduate education and faculty research in energy-related fields. At the very heart of university research is the faculty-student relationship, which not only brings the vitality of youth into the research process, but also guarantees a continuing infusion of well-trained specialists and leaders into the energy community. This element is critical to the nation's ability to meet the extraordinary demands that will be posed in the coming decades for people highly trained in the energy-related sciences.

- The Department should support interdisciplinary energy programs

173

and studies. A growing number of energy research problems requires an integrated approach and participation of several disciplines, including technical, environmental, and social sciences. The university is a uniquely suitable milieu for such work, not only because of the availability of many disciplines, but also because of the importance of interdisciplinary education in the training of energy specialists.

- The Department of Energy should look to leadership in energy research wherever it is found. Universities should be allowed, and encouraged, to compete on an equal footing with federally supported institutions for support from an augmented DOE basic research program, independent of how it is organized or managed.
- The Department should encourage and support cooperative basic research programs and high-level research coordination among universities, federal laboratories, and industry. Each member of this unique American "research triangle" has important contributions to make to the work of the others, and an enhanced symbiotic relationship among them will substantially increase the effectiveness of the entire national energy program.
- Universities should work with DOE to develop appropriate organizational forms, and be prepared to be accountable for the quality and effectiveness of DOE-sponsored research.
- The government should support an energy-related basic research program whose size and scope are commensurate with that of the energy problem. Fossil energy, solar energy, and energy conservation appear today to be key elements of a goal-oriented basic research effort needed to complement work in the nuclear field. We should, however, not repeat history and allow the nation's basic research effort to focus too narrowly around one or a few currently favored technologies. The best guide to what is right in basic research is, as always, the choices of the most creative minds in each field.

AAU ENERGY ADVISORY COMMITTEE

Jack M. Hollander, Associate Director, Lawrence Berkeley Laboratory, University of California (*Chairman*)

Frederick Abernathy, Professor, Division of Applied Sciences, Harvard University

174

John Baldeschweiler, Dean, Physical Sciences, California Institute of Technology

R. Steven Berry, Professor, Department of Chemistry, University of Chicago

Norman Bradburn, Associate Dean, Social Science, University of Chicago

D. Allan Bromley, Professor, Wright Nuclear Structure Laboratory, Yale University

Dale Compton, Vice-President, Ford Motor Company

James F. Crow, Professor, Department of Genetics, University of Wisconsin

Floyd R. Culler, Jr., President, Electric Power Research Institute

Edward David, Jr., President, Exxon Research and Engineering

Charles Engman, Associate Director, Institute of Environmental Studies, University of Wisconsin

William Fisher, Professor, Geological Sciences, University of Texas

James Fletcher, Professor, Technology and Energy Resources, University of Pittsburgh

Ronald Geballe, Dean, Graduate School, University of Washington

James Gibbons, Professor, Department of Electrical Engineering, Stanford University

Edwin L. Goldwasser, Acting Vice-Chancellor for Academic Affairs, University of Illinois

R. Eugene Goodson, Director, Institute for Interdisciplinary Studies, Potter Engineering Center, Purdue University

Julius Heldman, Vice-President, Shell Chemical Company

Richard Herson, Vice-President/Regional General Manager, Xerox Corporation

Charles Hosler, Dean, College of Earth and Mineral Science, Pennsylvania State University

Richard D. Jackson, Vice-President, Office of Business and Administration, Ohio State University

Charles O. Jones, Professor, Department of Political Science, University of Pittsburgh

Robert Kates, Professor, Graduate School of Geography, Clark University

Milton Katz, Professor, School of Law, Harvard University

Donald Kerr, Director, Los Alamos Scientific Laboratory

William Kerr, Director, Office of Energy Research, University of Michigan

Tjalling Koopmans, Professor, Cowles Foundation for Research in Economics, Yale University

Eugene E. Likens, Professor, Section of Ecology and Systematics, Division of Biological Sciences, Cornell University

Peter Likens, Dean, Engineering, Columbia University

Walter E. Massey, Director, Argonne National Laboratory

Denton Morrison, Professor, Department of Sociology, Michigan State University

William D. Nordhaus, Professor, Department of Economics, Yale University

Herman Postma, Director, Oak Ridge National Laboratory

Don Rice, The Rand Corporation

Arthur H. Rosenfeld, Professor, Department of Physics, University of California

Marc Ross, Professor, Department of Physics, University of Michigan

Roland Schmitt, Vice-President for Corporate Research and Development, General Electric Company

Carl M. Shy, Professor, Department of Public Health, University of North Carolina

David L. Sills, Executive Associate, Social Sciences Research Council

Robert Socolow, Professor, Mechanical and Aerospace Engineering, Princeton University

Roger Staehle, Dean, Institute of Technology, University of Minnesota

David White, Director, Energy Laboratory, Massachusetts Institute of Technology

International Business and International Studies: Prospects and Mutual Benefit
STAFF PAPER

THE RELATIONSHIP OF INTERNATIONAL, OR TRANSNATIONAL, STUDIES, foreign languages, and international business is the topic of this paper. Previous investigations have been made by such organizations as the American Council on Education, the American Assembly of Collegiate Schools of Business, and the now defunct Education and World Affairs. These efforts proceeded from the assumption that there is a direct utility of language and area studies skills for corporations operating overseas and that preparation of students in professional schools of business administration is incomplete without some form of internationalization. Although multinational corporations have supported these efforts in concept, they have not appreciably tapped university resources in practice. The purpose of this paper is to address the several reasons why this match has not been fully realized and to analyze and make recommendations for enhancing these critical relationships.

The concerns in international business and transnational studies derive from a number of political and economic facts. Recent record-setting trade deficits, the declining value of the dollar in international markets, inflation, reduced productivity, and a suspected diminution of innovative capacity have all helped to create an environment in the United States favorable to a renewed focus on international business generally and on export promotion in particular. These economic facts place increased national expectations on business, while the U.S. government is presently in the midst of a number of policy considerations that might assist in easing international business operations. Through a more open trade atmosphere being proposed by the Multilateral Trade Negotiations of the General Agreement on Trade and Tariffs, the Carter Administration and Congress are concentrating on reducing disincentives to trade, renewing and revising the Export Administration Act, and taking measures to promote exports by small- and medium-sized firms. One thrust of this paper is that relevant university expertise should be factored into this effort.

Exhortations directed at U.S. firms to increase exports cannot easily be legislated. An inertia that keeps many U.S. firms rooted only in the domestic economy is a result, in part, of ethnocentric attitudes and, in part, of fragmented and often restrictive U.S. government policy. The challenge is to maintain economic leadership through the stimulation and harnessing of untapped resources both in business and academe. A first critical need is to instill a national export consciousness to raise awareness of the benefits and necessity of exporting; a second is to find practical ways of making this happen. The working hypothesis of this paper is that mutually beneficial ways and means can be devised to harness university and other resources and capabilities to the manpower and information needs of U.S. business.

One of the classic problems in exploring the relationship of academe and business—government must be factored in as well—is that, except in the most ad hoc fashion, there are simply no established lines of communication between the three principals on this issue. Motivations of each group to act in established ways and to raise the possibility of new but related activities are identified. Findings on the utility of language and area studies in the hiring of U.S. international firms corroborate past studies; they are "pluses" but mostly secondary to functional business skills of accounting, marketing, finance, and so forth. Despite this fact, other productive relationships could be explored and constructed in mutually beneficial ways by realistically exploiting the strengths and needs of each sector.

This staff paper, originating with Samuel L. Hayden, managing director, Council of the Americas, and Leslie W. Koepplin, director, federal relations, and adjunct faculty member, Graduate School of Business Administration, Rutgers—The State University of New Jersey, was modified for purposes of the Business–Higher Education Forum.

Some portions of this paper appeared as part of a 1979 report to the President's Commission on Foreign Language and International Studies.

The opinions and recommendations in this paper are not intended to represent the official policy of the Business–Higher Education Forum or the American Council on Education.

BUSINESS

Methodology for analyzing the current and possible ways that corporations utilize university resources and expertise was to design a simple guide for personal and telephone interviews of a small, select group of corporations. The corporations include American International, American Medical International, Bank of America, DuPont, Exxon, Ford, General Electric, GTE, Morrison-Knudsen, Parsons, Sears, Security Pacific National Bank, Westinghouse, and Whittaker. The interviews by no means represent a statistically valid sample of U.S. business. The goal was to get a sense of what is being done in utilizing university resources and what might be possible, recognizing motivating factors of both business executives and academics.

Interviews led to a generalized profile of current collaboration between business and academe. *None* of the interviewed firms had ever hired a person at entry level specifically because of his or her foreign language or area studies background. Corporations usually worry about language and acculturation preparation of executives for overseas assignments only shortly before the actual physical move is to be made. The lead time varies according to the company and specific circumstances. Such preparation is contracted through specialized organizations like Berlitz, the Business Council for International Understanding, the Overseas Briefing Associates, and others. University language programs are not sought, much less used, because they are believed to be neither specialized nor flexible. Furthermore, the international operations of U.S. firms reflect the belief that English is the language of international business. And, although all corporations reported that fewer U.S. nationals are being sent abroad because of the incredible expense (often 2.5 times a U.S. salary), English is still seen as the dominant language. U.S. firms, therefore, have a high interest in hiring foreign students studying in this country, and often track their academic careers in order to be able to make job offers directly to them. Although foreign language skills are not seen as unimportant (many business representatives are fluent in other languages), it would be difficult to measure the cost-effectiveness of a firm's overseas business as a result of some hypothetical investment in language training.

The interviews also revealed little history of internships for students or faculty and almost no reliance on faculty research that is factored into corporate information systems. Most large corporations generate their own research at the headquarters and in the field offices. Facets of corporate activity are studied as social, economic, or political phenomena, but rarely is Ph.D.-level research fed into the corporate decision-making process. That is not the purpose of university research. Therefore, it is perhaps natural that there would be a poor fit between university research capacities and corporate needs for this kind of service.

The firms interviewed are mostly among the "Fortune 500" corporations. Although it is perhaps evident, it bears repeating that U.S. international corporations should not be viewed as monolithic or uniform in behavior. For example, some new-to-international-market financial institutions are forecasting tremendous growth overseas, while more experienced banks are seeing a leveling off of growth; some firms are efficiency seeking through integrated operations worldwide, while others are resource seeking; some are predominantly exporters from the United States, while others manufacture in host country markets to service local consumption or for export to third countries; some are mainly exporters, while others are direct investors. Often individual firms incorporate many of these facets simultaneously. In addition, sectoral differences occur whereby engineering and construction firms have different concerns and behavior than do service, agribusiness, or manufacturing firms. Approaches for linking university or other resources to international business should therefore recognize these essential differences.

At the headquarters level, international divisions of corporations are generally organized on a regional basis, as are many international studies units on campuses. As in universities, some regions are more important than others for corporations. U.S. foreign direct investment, according to the Department of Commerce, is roughly $150 billion. Approximately 80 percent of that total has been directed to Canada, Japan, Western Europe, and other industrialized countries. Of the remaining 20 percent, that in developing countries, roughly four-fifths is in Latin America. Even here, the concentration is in a few countries such as Mexico and Brazil. As an indication of concentration, the Commerce Department has projected that $3.7 billion of new plant and equipment will be placed in Latin America by U.S. firms in 1979, $1.7 billion of which will be in Brazil alone. These numbers reflect the relative unimportance of Africa, as compared with Latin America, when it comes to U.S. business activity.

Nonetheless, there is an increasingly stronger relationship between developing countries and the United States in total trade. In 1977, developing countries bought more than a third of all our exports. During the 1970s U.S. sales to developing countries grew 22 percent annually compared with 15 percent to industrialized countries. The potential for trade with communist countries, with perhaps the exception of the People's Republic of China, will probably continue to be limited. Again, although these figures can be refined, they do suggest that differentiation is important, that African studies programs, as one example, are relatively less attractive to business than are Latin American studies, which focus on a more financially compelling world area.

Firms looking for overseas opportunities generally export products before they invest abroad. A profile of U.S. exporting firms is revealing. Except for a core of large, high-powered corporations, U.S. firms are generally tied to a domestic orientation. The size, stability, and wealth of the U.S. market have not necessitated an international push. According to the Department of Commerce and as reported in *The New York Times*, 100 firms account for 50 percent of U.S. exports, 250 firms generate 80 percent of U.S. exports. In its effort to increase small- and medium-sized firm investment abroad, the Overseas Private Investment Corporation has determined that 8,000 firms with net sales less than $100 million (i.e., not in the "Fortune 1000" list) engage in exporting. In all, these firms probably account for the remaining 20 percent of U.S. export sales. Another way of putting into perspective the highly concentrated structure of U.S. international business is to recognize that a recently proposed, but rejected, merger of the Chamber of Commerce of the United States and the National Association of Manufacturers would have resulted in an association of more than 50,000 members.

The firms interviewed are part of a structure that aggressively looks to overseas markets. This kind of structure suggests two separate, but not necessarily mutually exclusive, approaches for linking university resources and programs to international business. One is geared to the large firms whose expertise and involvement in international matters are great. Another attempts to service small- and medium-sized firms in need of technical assistance and specific studies to become internationally directed. It is clear that the market concept needs to be applied to the university-business relationship because the diversity within business is certainly as great or greater than the diversity in the universities. For example, an "export awareness" education program could effectively utilize universities but need not be so directed to the 250 highly motivated export firms. Rather, the program would be geared to the large number of small- and medium-sized firms and to the public generally. If this analysis is correct, then it is perhaps also time that national, centralized solutions promoted by government programs and incentives must account for these differences in a way that induces localized or regional initiatives.

Another set of factors is also important and potentially beneficial in linking persons within business to the universities. Corporations often link themselves on a regional, state, or city basis to various associations. World trade clubs, foreign trade associations, councils on foreign relations, chambers of commerce, state departments of commerce, and specific international regional groupings often serve as surrogates and forums for certain kinds of activities. These groupings have not been adequately utilized by universities as means of initiating contact with corporations or of exploring possible joint program development. They represent an important resource for universities, as well as for individual firms.

Most corporations understand the need for international awareness among their employees. The difficulty is to find the time and the incentive mechanisms to make such awareness a reality. In a sense, large firms need much less attention than the multitude of small firms that have little international awareness and literally no export experience. Both tracks of business can be linked in various ways to university resources.

INTERNATIONAL STUDIES

The survey of international business found very little corporate use of international academic resources at American universities. There appear to be six major internal university reasons for this lack of relationship between international studies and international business: (1) America's international studies capacities are relatively new—most date only from the early 1960s; (2) there is a lack of funds for curriculum innovation involving foreign language and area studies, international business studies, and international business; (3) the internal campus reward system does not facilitate communication among foreign language and area studies, the schools of business and international business; (4) there are problems within the schools of business regarding international business education; (5) there is no forum for systematic, sustained communication between practitioners of international studies and international business; and (6) there is no real delivery capacity in U.S. business schools functionally geared to emerging business needs.

Much of America's international studies capacities, particularly in non-western areas of Africa, Latin America, and the Near East, are less than thirty years old. This capacity was created in the early 1960s through internal campus resources, including tuition, endowment funds, and state appropriations for the public universities, augmented by external sources that included foundations and the federal government. The Ford Foundation contributed approximately $300 million to this effort and the federal government, through the National Defense Education Act (NDEA) Title VI legislation, has provided a level close to $250 million of funding since 1958. The Ford Foundation terminated its funding in 1968 at a time when the international resources had finally been solidified in campus budgets, but where there was no clear sense of how these new resources could be related to international business. This period also marked the start of general university budget constraints from state and federal sources. Funding under NDEA Title VI has not filled that void. In terms of 1958 dollars, inflation has taken a heavy toll on federal funding of academic institutions. There has simply been no new funding available for experimentation in curriculum design and innovation between international studies and international business. It is important to note that even in the heyday of foundation and federal funding, political and academic need, not economic need, triggered support.

The U.S. Department of Education's funding of foreign language and area studies under NDEA Title VI legislation provides an excellent profile of universities that have substantial international studies capacities. In order to qualify for federal funding, which is awarded on a nationally competitive basis, a university must have an internally funded base of faculty appointments in a variety of departments, supplemented by staff and library resources in various geographical areas, specifically Africa, the Near East, East Africa, South and Southeast Asia, the Soviet Union and Eastern Europe, and Latin America. Some 60 percent of the funds are awarded to twelve universities: U. C. Berkeley, UCLA, Chicago, Columbia, Harvard, Illinois, Indiana, Michigan, Stanford, Washington, Wisconsin, and Yale. Furthermore, within these dozen universities, the overwhelming majority of international studies resources is concentrated in the humanities and the social sciences. Professor Richard Lambert, in his well-known survey of 1970, noted the disparity in numbers between the language instructors, historians, and political scientists on one hand and the economists on the other. We have detected no measurable shifts since then. We think it fair to say that what this collection of twelve large prestigious universities does best, particularly in the humanities and social sciences, is research oriented to graduate training, particularly at the Ph.D. level. In addition, the faculties of these universities have a reward system firmly based in the disciplines. It is here that professional stature, tenure, and promotion are earned. These interrelated factors—the mission of the Ph.D.-granting institutions in the humanities and social sciences and the faculty reward system—provide very little impetus to establish and maintain contact with either the schools of business or the international business community.

The international dimension of the schools of business has been the subject of a recent excellent survey by Professor Lee Nehrt under the auspices of the American Council on Education. The survey found a lack of attention to the international area in the entire business curriculum. Some 75 percent of the recently graduated Ph.D.s and D.B.A.s, who represent the business faculty of the future, had no international course work at all; an additional 10 percent had only one course. In addition, the Nehrt survey found a need to review the undergraduate business curriculum and the need to design innovative international programs directed toward the nontraditional mid-career student. The survey's prime recommendation was for the creation of a series of faculty seminars directed toward establishing an international component in each of the traditional functional areas of business education, such as accounting, finance, marketing, and business policy. The first of these seminars, funded by General Electric, was held in 1978. In addition, the American Assembly of Collegiate Schools of Business has recently mandated that any school of business that wishes to receive or maintain accreditation status must carry an international component in its curriculum.

The important point to emphasize here is the newness of these developments (the Nehrt report appeared in 1977). Typically, a faculty member from a foreign language department, concerned about dropping enrollments, walks across campus to the School of Business and finds neither international ability nor interest.

The last point is that there is no mechanism for sustained, systematic communication between the interested parties. Academics, particularly in the humanities and social sciences, very often do not have good contacts in the business community. They do not know which firms might have personnel requirements that could draw on their students; likewise, business has no central point of reference to survey the academic community for some indication of mutual gain. There is simply no one place where America's international studies and America's international business interests come together in a long-term, systematic way. In some instances, there is more than a lack of communication—there is what amounts to mutual mistrust.

GOVERNMENT

The U.S. government operates in many ways to affect both business and academe. For better or worse, the government is in fact an intimate partner of both. New policy directions through incentives and disincentives are formulated on a continuing basis to control and redirect many activities.

Literally every business executive, when given the opportunity, decries the seemingly increased intervention of government in the daily international operations of private enterprise. Many executives feel that any positive business development initiatives of the government are more than offset by disincentives or policies that hamstring business. Despite their original good intentions, regulatory practices have had a detrimental effect on corporate competitiveness internationally. Some examples are increased personal tax liability on U.S. citizens working abroad, inadequate and untimely export licensing procedures, inadequate export financing, boycott legislation, human rights legislation, inadequate embassy support services, and increased paperwork and reporting requirements. Most corporations feel that their competitiveness is reduced because of these "restrictive" policies. They also feel that foreign firms have a distinct advantage given the positive incentives they receive from their own governments.

Although the government, particularly the U.S. Department of Commerce, has appointed several task forces to study the loose system of disincentives as well as new ways to promote exports, it is not clear how new initiatives would be constructed or coordinated. One concern is that if U.S. economic and business presence is reduced abroad, corporations will not be a source of growth for area studies and language programs in universities. On the other hand, without forging links between university resources and corporations, we will never know the measurable productive relationship between the two.

The personal tax liability of U.S. corporate personnel abroad is particularly troublesome. Unofficial estimates of the number of Americans abroad in corporate activity are revealing. Sears International has roughly 24,000 employees abroad, of whom only about sixty are Americans; in General Electric 500 of 110,000 abroad are Americans. These two examples are indicative of the enormous expense that must be incurred to station Americans abroad. They also tell why foreign students in the United States are so attractive to corporations; these students are as well educated as Americans and do not require foreign language and host country acculturation training; they are also much less expensive given the U.S. tax consideration. The long-range effect of this kind of tendency needs to be assessed, but it is perhaps not premature to conclude that for such firms the foreign student is simply much more valuable than the American student for international operations and that international studies are not as important as they could be. In some nations, it is also politically wiser to do this given national sensitivities and restrictions in obtaining work visas.

The federal government has provided money to assist in the internationalization of universities, as have several corporations. It is now considering ways to increase U.S. exports. In both cases, incentives have been the key to prompting action. These incentives usually are seen as investments in future actions and performance. New government policies and support can help to create new relationships between university and corporate resources, thereby leading to the attainment of broader national objectives. These objectives are qualitative as well as quantitative. For example, for FY 1980 and 1981, U.S. foreign assistance will total less than $9 billion annually, while U.S. foreign direct investment will probably exceed $170 billion. Business diplomacy is perhaps as important as state diplomacy, a fact that needs to be recognized by the U.S. government, U.S. academic institutions, and U.S. business.

The two tracks need emphasis. Large, experienced international firms will increase their effectiveness overseas more through reduced government regulation than by any kind of immediate ties to universities. However, the cultural, political, and economic expertise available in universities has the potential for assisting long-range and strategic planning for the large firms. Organization and effective delivery mechanisms for such expertise need to be explored. Small, inexperienced domestic firms need both financial and technical assistance from the government and other sources to induce them to enter international markets. Smaller firms also have compounded problems because they are subject to the same regulation as large firms. In each case, however, universities could play specific but different roles. Export promotion by small inexperienced internationally aspiring firms will not come about by Small Business Administration loans or by government pleas. These, coupled with other factors including university resources, will be needed for such an effect to be accomplished.

RECOMMENDATIONS

The recommendations that follow recognize three primary actors: higher education, business, and government. At various times, all three have addressed the question of the role of international studies in international business. The reality is that there is precious little precedent of international business' use of international studies' information and personnel. Despite this lack of precedent, colleges and universities have argued that international studies are in the national interest and deserve national support. If the argument continues to be used, there must be recognition that international business is a significant part of the national interest. The recognition has perhaps always been made at least tacitly, but now it is more important because of international economic problems and the necessity of greater business performance both here and abroad. The following recommendations derive from our working hypothesis that an unrealized potential exists between business and academe and that the government can provide the incentives and funds to explore these new relationships.

Recommendations for government programs

The Business–Higher Education Forum could support improved government programs in this area, and business and higher education could move independently of the government for mutual benefit. First, recommendations for government action:

1. *Study centers.* That the U.S. Department of Education funding for the traditional foreign language and area studies centers be increased and that these funds be earmarked for international business and economic studies. Department policy should require, whenever possible, the involvement of international business subject matters in these centers—both in the guidelines for center competition and in the subsequent programs. Each recipient of funds should be required to appoint an Academic/Business Advisory Council.

2. *International business studies.* That the U.S. Department of Education fund at least four innovative undergraduate and four graduate programs in international business studies each year for the next five years at a minimum level of $100,000 each. The focus of the undergraduate programs should be either in developing international components for the undergraduate core business curriculum in accounting, finance, marketing, and business policy or in augmenting traditional undergraduate curriculum preparation for the international M.B.A. student. The focus of the innovative graduate programs should be in the development of new international programs for the nontraditional mid-career or part-time student.

3. *Internships.* That the government support the creation of a system of internships for students directed toward an international business career. These could be funded in either of two ways: the use of federally supported fellowships to work in this area or the creation of a simple system of tax incentives for participating firms based on new expenditures for international business personnel.

4. *Metropolitan study centers.* That the U.S. Department of Education and the U.S. Department of Commerce fund at least five major centers of international business studies and research in America's major metropolitan areas that have heavy involvement in international studies and international business. These five centers, perhaps located in World Trade Centers, the Conference Board, or similar organizations, would be funded on an experimental basis for at least three years at a level of $300,000 each. Their mission would be threefold:

a. they would serve as a clearinghouse for international studies-international business exchange;

b. they would disseminate information on international business potential and on successful joint programs between business and academe; and

c. they would serve as a forum for the discussion and development of government policy on international business and international studies.

This recommendation is designed to cover a multitude of needs expressed by business executives and academicians in interviews with them. In the first instance, many of the business people were surprised to learn that American universities have extensive resources in international studies; most did not know what foreign language and area studies centers are. A clearinghouse of information available on international studies resources could be a first step in an attempt to alert potential users of this resource.

Most important, a clearinghouse could provide a systematic forum for continuing business-academic-government discussions on needs and policies. International business is by nature flexible and changing; its information and operating needs also change; its personnel needs, therefore, also change. A clearinghouse could do much to establish a base for the kind of communication between the three groups that is crucial to a future increased U.S. role in the international economy.

5. *Small business.* That the Small Business Administration and the Department of Commerce fund a network of Small Business Development Centers (SBDCs) throughout the country. The SBDCs could be modeled after the land-grant system for agriculture development and extension in each state. The purpose of each center would be to bring together as many useful resources as are possible to help develop and revitalize small- and medium-sized firms. Export assistance and export education, along with domestic concerns, would be functions of these centers. The resources at the centers could include university faculty and students, state departments of commerce, experts from exporting firms, retired executives from the International Executive Service Corps, and others. Activities, in addition to direct technical assistance to participating firms, could include studies in government policy on small- and medium-sized businesses, market opportunity surveys, university curriculum design, entrepreneurship studies, and others. Methods of operation to carry out these activities

and functions could include team studies and technical assistance done by students under the direction of faculty and business participants.

Recommendations for business–higher education action

Until the establishment of the Business–Higher Education Forum, there was no formal mechanism for establishing mutually beneficial, long-term linkages between the substantial international interests of both universities and corporations, among other agenda items. Various professional groups have been organized to deal with specialized issues, business advisory boards have been formed to help guide academic efforts, and study groups and conferences have focused on aspects of these relationships. But few initiates have endured with a sufficiently broad gauge or with enough prestige to cause widespread change. Considering that America's colleges and universities maintain the greatest resources in international studies in the world and that American firms have been the world leaders in international business during this century, the Forum's interest in international dimensions seems most opportune.

It is the thesis of these recommendations that a mutually beneficial relationship between international business and international studies is possible only through a systematic, sustained commitment at the highest levels to communication and program experimentation. And this relationship can be encouraged through the Business–Higher Education Forum. This paper has identified the factors in international business and international studies which bear on such a relationship.

Following are specific proposals. They include, first, financial goals and an administrative structure as part of an effort to increase the level of resources available for international education. Second, they include three project proposals that the Forum could consider implementing as part of its action agenda in the international area.

1. *Financial Goals and Administrative Structure.* There is little doubt that every academic member of the Forum is capable of designing specific international programs that would be of immediate interest to business. There is also little doubt that business will neither appreciate nor understand international studies until some more substantial efforts are undertaken in this area. However, none of this is

190

going to happen under currently available resources. New initiatives entail new costs. Specifically, the Forum could:

a. identify the business leaders who have the most interest in international business and recommend that they commit resources and staff time annually to work with universities in developing international business–international studies programs.

b. identify the academic leaders who have the most interest in international studies and recommend that they commit resources or in-kind contributions annually for the same purpose.

c. recommend that the Secretary of Education set aside funds from the discretionary monies available under NDEA Title VI legislation (sections 602 and 603) for research in curriculum improvements in international business studies, with particular emphasis on undergraduate preparation for international business training and nontraditional graduate training and for "outreach monies" for innovative programs in serving business needs. A half million dollars a year would launch these efforts.

d. maximize the resources identified above by addressing certain administrative questions. The Forum could create a standing committee to identify those already existing programs that involve international studies–international business cooperation and are of potential significant interest to the Forum membership; work with the Director of the U.S. Department of Education's International Division to ensure that there is coordination between the efforts of the Business–Higher Education Forum and the efforts recommended for support under Titles 602 and 603 of NDEA Title VI legislation; and identify and make decisions of future program implementation on behalf of the Forum.

2. *Specific Projects.* The proposals that follow offer a variety of international activities in which the Forum could become engaged. They are not meant to be seen as a "package," but to be critically reviewed as independent and separate activities. Each has several common characteristics. Each is experimental and can test some of the assumptions about business-university relations; each is designed to address specific problems and goals; and each is intended to be in the self-interest of both universities and corporations. The focus here is on proposals that, if proven successful in implementation, would

provide an innovative multiplier effect through replication by other organizations and institutions.

a. *Student Internships.* An internship program for American students in U.S. international corporations would be useful for several reasons. It represents a simple mechanism for establishing communications and promoting mutual understanding. With proper, serious design, the project could accomplish much in reducing mistrust and suspicion on both sides. Students could clearly understand the potential for international business employment, and the corporations could explore the value of such projects, determine if additional projects are warranted, and evaluate this kind of project as a personnel screening device.

Objectives:
- increase understanding between the two sets of principals;
- contribute to economic and corporate literacy;
- give students practical experience; and
- give corporations a possible personnel tracking and screening device.

Suggested internship topics:
- the role and organization of sociopolitical analysis in corporate information systems;
- structure of in-house seminars for international executives;
- annotated bibliographies on key markets/regions;
- translation services;
- the utility to corporate decision making of university capability in political risk analysis;
- case studies of corporate citizenship;
- cost and effects of specific U.S. government regulation on firm's operations abroad; and
- benefits of U.S. corporate investment abroad.

b. *Environmental Analysis of One Country.* The Forum could consider a project that would attempt to define the relationship between campus knowledge in international studies and the corporate need for international information.

The project might be in the form of an analysis of one country in social, political, cultural, and economic terms. The country as a candidate for analysis could be Mexico, and there are several reasons for this choice. First, Mexico is foreign but so near that interdependence is the reality. Second, there is a set of seemingly insoluble problems, such as illegal immigration linked to other bilateral issues, that require greater attention than that paid by the government alone. The harnessing of all our potential resources could have a beneficial effect on public policy as well as business performance.

Universities do have a knowledge base and human resources relevant to country-specific understanding. While corporations do possess information about economic activity in a country, they may want to broaden their contextual information about a particular country or market.

This project is predicated on a positive response to the following questions about the utility of university resources to business needs: Is the information which universities possess in this area of use to corporations? If the answer is positive, how can this information be organized? If again the answer is positive, are universities willing to work with corporations to provide that information? Again if positive, are corporations willing to pay for the use of this information?

It appears that this relationship has not been systematically addressed by any organization in a sustained fashion. The development of environmental analyses of this sort would provide the Forum with a unique opportunity for additional future programming.

3. *Business-University Collaboration in Third World Countries.* As many businessmen have gained international expertise through overseas assignments, so many faculty at a number of universities have become internationalized by participating in institution building and technical assistance projects abroad. This route for faculty development and service is now relatively closed because funding is not available to U.S. universities.

Third World countries, through forums like the U.N. Conference on Science and Technology for Development, have identified the need for massive training and education at local levels. Because training and technical assistance are often integral parts of U.S. investment abroad, it can be assumed that in Latin America, for example, these are significant activities given the fact that U.S. direct investment in that region is approaching $30 billion.

The model borrowed for purposes here is Project Pace of the

American Chamber of Commerce of South Africa that has planned, designed, and started fund raising for the first vocational and recreational center in Soweto. Similar efforts could be undertaken in Third World countries, with groups of corporations acting as donors and joint venture partners and universities providing the technical assistance for the design and implementation of training centers.

Objectives:
- create a project that would serve manpower training needs of corporations in a Third World country; raise the level of manpower skills in that country; harness U.S. universities' capabilities while helping to internationalize faculty;
- help meet critical need in developing countries while serving the interests of U.S. corporations and universities; and
- go beyond the corporate donor–university recipient relationship by involving relevant corporate personnel in project design and implementation.

CONCLUSION

The financial goals and administrative structure, as well as the project proposals just presented, provide the framework for future action by business and higher education on their roles in the international area. The belief that corporations and universities can increase interaction in mutually beneficial ways needs to be substantiated by project experimentation; this the Business–Higher Education Forum seems in a unique position to undertake. There is much to gain nationally and transnationally with relatively little investment in time and money.